How to SURVIVE the Coming RETIREMENT STORM

A 5-Step Process for Success in Volatile Times

Matchstick Literary
1-888-306-8885
orders@matchliterary.com

Here's what the readers say about the book:

"This one's a balanced and practical guide into living your best life after retirement. Some may find this book unnecessary but for me I find it to be truly helpful. It covers topics about handling your finances and dealing with your depression knowing you're about to end your career. The storyline did a wonderful job at explaining everything on the how's when your retirement approaches." - *Tricia Dorothy G. Paulsen*

"It's an inspiring and practical book on how to spend your retirement wisely. The author is extremely knowledgeable on the subject and he offers complex information that are quite relevant and easy to understand. He points out the essential points that are needed for people who are about to retire, reassuring them that it's not such a bad thing. I highly recommend this book to everyone who's nearing the retirement age, a good book indeed." - *Gilbert Ryan T. Zelinski*

"I think this book may serve as a perfect retirement gift for retirees. It's packed with wise advice,and it's whole heartedly written by Robert Margetic. If you are embarking on the retirement journey, give this book a shot! Even after retirement, there are still some exciting and more meaningful experiences life has to offer. I think retiring is the most rewarding phase of a man's life as you get to enjoy life to the fullest. The book is very engaging and there's just so much wisdom in it." - *Ronaldo M. Eriksson*

Contents

Part I
STRUCTURE

Chapter 1

THE COMING STORM

One thing you can count on in retirement is your experience will be different than your parent's and grandparent's. Theirs had a certain sense of predictability and reliability. Yours will be saddled with uncertainty and volatility.

If you are like most new retirees you live a grander lifestyle and hold loftier retirement ambitions than your parents. You likely will find your pension, if any and Social Security covers less of your retirement lifestyle. In turn, you will become more dependent on your savings.

As a new retiree you will live longer. You will need more money and it will need to last longer. Living longer also exposes you to more inflation and increases the chances of running up unexpected medical expenses.

Recent headlines show financial market meltdowns, housing crises, potential cuts to Social Security and Medicare, and debt flowing over the horizon along with riots over pension cuts in foreign lands. Large corporations file for bankruptcy to shed pension liabilities while cities and states consider doing the same.

Huge US budget deficits and massive debt will limit the government's ability to respond to increasing needs. The current U.S. debt is $30 trillion with states adding another $6 trillion. If history is a guide, unsustainable debt leads to a long period of negligible economic growth or rapid inflation. Many of the things you counted on for a successful retirement come into question.

Those facing retirement today are in a quandary. It is like they are putting together a puzzle without a picture and are not sure they have all of the pieces. Apprehension and worry abound. Fifty-five percent fear outliving their money, forty-five percent fear Alzheimer's disease and nursing homes, fifty-one percent feel they cannot maintain their lifestyle in retirement, while seventy-five percent state they are not prepared to manage retirement for thirty years.

80 Million People between ages 45-65 in the US are supplemented by 60 million more in Europe, Canada, Japan and Australia who face the same uncertain future. A tremendous number of people will place tremendous stress on an exhausted system. All of these events will crash together to create a storm of unknown magnitude and intensity.

The aftermath of the storm will alter the retirement landscape. In all likelihood those who saved will face higher taxes and cuts in Medicare and Social Security benefits. Some employer pension plans will be cut or frozen. Those who were unable to save or have inadequate savings will face lower government benefits and less help from employers resulting in a lower standard of living.

In all likelihood, you will face higher unexpected costs while becoming more dependent on your savings. Both, your expenses and income will be less certain and more volatile. More responsibility will be shifted to you testing your ability to balance uncertain expenses with unpredictable income. Those most capable of adaptation will survive.

You probably haven't retired before and can't count on your experience to serve as a guide. Yet, you have been through major life changes. You may have been married, managed a career and raised children. You began each without experience and relied on your wit and wherewithal to get you through.

By now you have accumulated a set of life experiences that surely qualifies you to manage your way through retirement. You have managed investments, expenses, relationships and life challenges. You have made it this far and with some guidance you can manage a successful retirement.

But what makes the retirement stage different from previous life stages? In previous stages you had the strength and vitality of youth coupled with expectations of increased income as you matured. This gave you a sense of confidence you could meet challenges head on.

You counted on your health. You could take on debt and drain your savings knowing you could replenish them over time. There was less a sense of urgency and time was on your side.

Now, you will enter retirement with less agility and more questions than confidence. In retirement economic uncertainty takes on new meaning. If you have ever been between jobs you know how different it feels to spend money when you don't have a job. Or imagine how you would feel if you were retired and your 401(k) tanked as it most likely did in 2007-08. You wonder how you will replace that lost wealth and lost income.

For some, this nagging uncertainty exposes a certain vulnerability that is difficult to articulate. You have dealt with uncertainty most of your adult life and can be expected to deal with what comes at you. However, the new retirement raises a new set of questions. Getting the answers right requires a new way of thinking and a new set of tools.

The old way of thinking guides traditional retirement planning. It is a long-term approach. The planning is anchored by a fixed estimate of inflation and an average return on investments. These numbers are straight-lined many years into the future to let you know if your savings plan is in the retirement ball park or if you have enough money to last the rest of your life.

Yet you know inflation will not be fixed and you will not earn the average return year-in-year-out. You know the numbers are wild guesses, but lacking alternatives you use them anyway.

You may think since you are projecting so far into the future so many other things can happen why not use this approach. This approach is valid as long as the time horizon is long and your emphasis is on planning. But, as you get closer to retirement or are retired, the flaws in this approach can be costly when your emphasis needs to shift from long term planning to short term management and control.

For example, let's say your plan assumes an average investment return. It may be a conservative number like 5%. This is surely a reasonable number based on historical returns in the financial markets. You may feel if you earn at least this much everything will be fine.

But an average return is misleading and can lead to a false sense of security. It is not the average return that is most important in retirement, but how much your return varies and in what order you get your returns.

You may average 5% over a ten-year period but if the first five years have negative returns or returns less than 5% and you are taking money out of your account, you may dig a hole so deep as to never recover.

Your expenses face a similar fate when something unexpected like a disability, a death of a spouse or a major expense like a new car or home repairs drain your budget. Once retired, there is a direct link between expenses and savings. If savings are drawn down to meet these unexpected expenses, you have less principal to produce future income.

The rigidity of planning for the old system will crack from stressors created by the retirement storm. Flexibility, agility and quick evaluation and response are the characteristics of storm survivors. The ability to measure, monitor and respond to changing events separates the successful from the clueless.

The old system is two generations old. The 3.0 version has yet to be developed. The government will tinker with the old system in attempts to get a few more years out of it. You are caught in the transition period between the old crumbling system and the yet-to-be defined system. This interim is the retirement storm. Its full impact is two to three years out but the ominous clouds are on the horizon. The time to begin preparations is today.

You need to place a new emphasis on the balance between expense and income. This requires you to manage your personal affairs and your investments in a different way. You will need to learn new ways to manage and control your retirement.

Interims between the phasing out old systems and creating new systems are necessarily volatile. The storm will be this transition period and your challenge will be to navigate through the storm. You will need to blend some of the old with some of the new while you continually adjust to your new retirement.

To be successful requires a new way of thinking and a new approach to guide you through the storm. You have the essential skills. You just need to refine and direct them more effectively.

As more responsibility shifts to you to generate your income, manage expenses and tend to your personal aging health needs two questions repeatedly will be asked: 1) how will change today impact the remainder of your retirement; and 2) what are you going to do about it.

This book provides you with the picture of the puzzle and ensures you have all of the pieces. It shows you how to use new tools and a new system to help you develop control over your retirement. Critical elements and their interaction will be organized, measured and evaluated. You will be able to mark actual and relative progress, make informed decisions and continually renew projections to guide you to a successful retirement.

Some of you will do the work your self. Others will hire someone else to do the work. Either way you need to understand how the pieces fit together and know what questions to ask should things go awry.

It is unclear if the storm will be one and done or if there are a series of storms ahead. Nevertheless, once the first storm passes through some of the things you currently take for granted will change. The outside forces agitated by the storm will affect how you live out your retirement dream and you need to plan for them.

Your retirement plan can't operate in isolation. Those outside forces will impact your assumptions, decisions and experiences. Before we get started let's look at some of those forces as they can provide perspective to better prepare you for the trip ahead.

Assumptions Matter

When you prepare for anything you need to assess the environment. When you design any plan you must make some guesses about the future. It is no different when planning for retirement. The assumptions you make reflect your perceptions and influence your decisions.

Assumptions are no more than educated guesses. Since we are guessing about the future it is less about being right then about being close. But the assumptions you make will affect how you spend and invest your money.

There are several primary assumptions you need to make to begin your plan. You need to determine: how long you will live, your investment return, an inflation rate, your lifestyle expenses, your health status, and tax rates.

One way to instantly achieve retirement success is to assume you have a large amount of savings, you will earn 20 percent on your investments, no inflation, moderate lifestyle expenses, superb health the rest of your life and declining tax rates. Once you plug in these assumptions your retirement suddenly looks bright.

This of course is nonsense since the assumptions are unreasonable. But what makes assumptions reasonable? A lower rate of return gets you closer. How much lower? What is a reasonable inflation rate? What about life's uncertainties?

The better you can refine your guesses the more confidence you will have in your plan. Most guesses about the future start with a look to the past. But, the storm will make the past look like an outdated travel guide. Greater emphasis must be placed on the near term.

To successfully navigate the storm's volatility your plan needs to be of a short-term nature. This would generally be two to three years out. Your plan also would be complemented by frequently measuring, monitoring and evaluating issues critical to your well being.

Since you likely will spend twenty to thirty years in retirement, you still will need a long- term perspective to provide guidance while you are attentively managing the short term. Certain long term demographic trends will bear on your decisions. If left disregarded, these trends can coerce you into weakened indefensible positions.

Your retired lifestyle will differ from your working lifestyle. The changes you anticipate mark your starting point. Your current outlook beyond your lifestyle needs to be adjusted by broader demographic trends. There are three broad demographic trends that will influence the quality of your retirement life:

1. Longevity
2. Age Wave
3. Declining birthrates

These trends will crest during your retirement. They will influence interest rates, market returns, inflation and your overall lifestyle. They need to be part of the back story of your retirement picture.

Longevity - Much is bantered about life expectancy. A healthy baby born in the US can expect to live to age 77.4. However, if you make it to age 65, men can expect to live an additional 16.3 years and women 19.2. But the life expectancy number is calculated using mortality numbers.

If the US experiences an inordinate number of infant mortalities or if some killer flu attacks a wide swath of the population, or if auto accidents or homicides increase among younger people the life expectancy number declines.

This leads to the irrational conclusion where if a large number of younger people die, you, as an older person, die sooner as your calculated life expectancy shortens. Life expectancy becomes a dubious number for planning how long your resources need to last once you retire. A more reasonable assumption of how long you expect to live helps you to plan to not outlive your resources.

A Danish study of twins showed genes accounted for 25 percent of longevity. This leaves us to speculate the other 75% is influenced by environment, behavior and luck. The leading cause of death in those over age 65 is heart disease – 32%, followed by cancer – 22% and strokes – 8%.

Medical science shows you can do something about the leading causes of death. You can extend your life through proper diet and exercise. You can choose to improve your environment by moving to a healthier place and since you made it this far, you have some degree of luck.

Your thinking needs to shift from life expectancy to lifespan. Life expectancy is the average number of years you are expected to live. Life span is the genetically determined length of life. Many scientists believe this number is between 100-115 years.

If you are healthy and active at age 65 you likely may live thirty or more years in retirement. This necessitates a change in the way you view how you will manage your time and resources as you now can be expected to live the complete human lifecycle.

Obviously, a longer life requires more money. You will spend more and what you spend your money on will increase in price through the ravages of inflation. The fixed dollar amount of savings at retirement will need to be managed to last longer exposing you to the additional investment risks.

Living longer also increases the chances that more years are spent with health problems and disabilities. Longevity adds complexity to retirement. You will need to be more attentive to change and quicker in response.

Most healthy retirees plan to age 90 or better yet 95. In addition to how long your money needs to last, how long you think you will live also determines the best choices for pension, annuity and Social Security payments.

Age wave - This identifies the massive number of baby boomers crashing through life. Visually, it has been likened to a snake swallowing a raccoon or a tsunami crashing onto shore. Current estimates show 4-5 million of us will retire each year for the next 20 years. These 80 million people will change aging in unforeseen ways complicating how you plan for retirement.

Not all of these future retirees saved enough to fund their retirement. Only twelve percent of the new retirees have savings in excess of $500,000. The average savings available to invest is $125,000.

This implies many people have saved less than the average amount. But, even if we assume someone who saved the average amount managed it prudently, they could reasonably expect an additional $350 per month to supplement their Social Security.

Social Security itself was never intended to provide 100% of retirement income. It was intended to supplement personal savings and employer pensions. Those relying solely on Social Security will find their monthly benefit leaves them living below the poverty level.

This could cause a split between retirees who saved and those who did not, or were unable to for various reasons. This rift has the potential to be exploited politically with uncertain outcomes. Nevertheless, one likely outcome would be higher taxes and lower benefits for those who saved.

The *age wave* will affect the value of savings and investments. As people retire, they will tend to reduce the amount of money invested in stocks and other growth assets. This selling pressure will tend to push down the value of growth assets as savings are shifted towards income assets.

Though income assets may go up in value the increase will be offset by the lower value of growth assets and by lower real interest rates as more money competes for the same pool of income assets. The end result is likely to be lower monthly income from your savings.

Home prices will also face downward pressure as retirees in mass seek to tap home equity, move to smaller residences or move to a different locale. The increase in homes for sale may have a similar effect on home prices as the foreclosure mess of 2007-2009 when home prices dropped precipitously.

Declining birth rates - The US and the rest of the developed world have seen its birthrates decline. Current birthrates are 1.6 per woman which are less than replacement rates. Birthrates are also declining in developing countries as infant mortality lessens and economic opportunities favor fewer children.

Absent women opting to have more children and large increases in immigration, the population decline will tend to lower economic growth as a lower population lessens demand for a variety of goods and services. Companies will struggle for workers pushing wages and prices up. New markets may become harder to find threatening the viability of certain companies and industries.

Old retirees had roughly fifteen workers supporting each retiree when Social Security began. This number dropped to three workers in the 1980s. Old retirees had confidence their Social Security benefits would be maintained and even increased. You as a new retiree face closer to one worker supporting each retiree.

Social Security and Medicare are funded through payroll taxes. The trustees of those programs reported in 2009 that Social Security will run out of money within 20 years and Medicare within 5 years. Social Security reported its first deficit in recent times in 2009.

Worse yet, there is no cash in the Social Security trust fund, just IOUs. Where will the government get the cash to send you your monthly benefit? Most likely they will get it by issuing more debt. You will be creditor of the US government just like China and other debt holders.

Existing workers would need to pay 3-5 times the current amount in payroll taxes to fund these IOUs or the government will need to find new funding and/or reduce benefits. If the deficits are funded solely by payroll taxes this would push them to over 20% which would increase inflation and lower US global competitiveness.

A shortage of workers tends to result in higher wages. This may be especially true in service industries like health care and professional services. The end result will be higher prices for retirees seeking these services as their inflation rate exceeds the average inflation rate for all goods and services. The higher prices will combine with longer waits for desired services.

Less people in subsequent generations will lower demand for houses exasperating new retirees seeking to sell their homes for their desired price. A reduced number of workers will be contributing to 401(k) s and other growth assets tempering long term rates of return.

New retirees with no children or few children will have less family help available as they age. Those who can afford it will pay for additional domestic services while others will depend on government or go without.

These trends need not be ominous as opportunities are bound to arise. Nevertheless, these trends need to be factored into your assumptions of how your retirement will play out. As you look at the assumptions you will make remember small percentage differences compounded over time result in large dollar differences.

For example, if you were to earn 5% on $100,000 compounded for thirty years you end up with $432,190. If you earned 6% you end up with $574,350; quite a difference. Similarly, the impact of 2% inflation increases your annual expenses over thirty years from $30,000 to $54,342. If inflation were 3% you would need $72,819 to maintain your lifestyle.

These demographic changes on the whole will tend to lower your investment returns and increase your living expenses. As you can see, small percentage changes can have a big impact on your lifestyle. This further emphasizes the need for a more agile and responsive approach to planning, managing and controlling your retirement.

History is a good starting point, but you need to make a storm assessment and you need to modify your outlook by these demographic trends if you are to have confidence in your retirement plan.

The New Retirement Environment

Take a snapshot of where you are today. You know your mortgage or monthly rent payment, how much you spend on food, who you hang out with, your state of health and where your savings are invested.

Fast forward and you may find a package of your favorite snack has gone from $1.89 to $2.69 a package, your best friend moved, your back pain now shoots down your leg and your mutual fund has lost money each of the last three months.

What do you do? You will likely notice this is a two-part problem. One part is the result of your actions and the other part is caused by outside forces. You might be able to switch snacks, make a new friend, stop playing tennis and move your investments around. These actions may make you feel you are doing something but how do you know if you have resolved your problems or just created a new set of problems?

Recognizing this is as a two-part problem is the beginning of gaining control over your retirement. What you decide to do is one control lever you have in your retirement plan. The second is a strategy to manage the impact of outside forces.

You can get a sense of what you will do and what is happening around you by taking in the big picture of your retirement environment, the 40,000 foot view. From this perspective you can see what you will be doing and if any new storms are approaching.

There is a different lifestyle cost if you choose to travel extensively, go to culinary school or study the flora and fauna in the rainforest than there is in babysitting the grandchildren and occasionally taking them to an amusement park. Your decisions have impact.

What you do with your free time, where you live, what you drive and who you socialize with all play a role in the cost of your overall lifestyle. Once you determine what you will do you can figure out the cost. Then, you can see if your savings can provide the necessary income.

But, to live a successful retirement requires you to attend to more than just financial matters. You could spend one quarter to one third of your life retired. The change from your working self to your retired self will compel you to figure out what to do with all of this new found time. You won't want to spend all of this time alone.

You can plan to meet the outside forces by anticipating likely events and readying actions to counter-act or take advantage of economic, political and social opportunities. Society will confront new demands on how best to accommodate an aging population. This will create ongoing change requiring you to frequently monitor your affairs and make adjustments if you are to stay in control.

Through all of this, you must find a way to take care of yourself personally, socially and financially. You need to develop a new mindset of how you see your retirement playing out. There are three things for you to think through:

1. What is your new life's role?
2. How do you perceive aging?
3. What is meant by financial security?

You will need a new way of thinking about the new retirement. The better you can articulate how you picture retirement, the better your plan. The better your plan is, the greater your ability to manage and control your retirement.

New Life Role

Retirement for the previous generation lasted on average ten years. Many of the old retirees worked physically intensive jobs. Their productivity waned with age. Most were unable to transfer work skills to new endeavors limiting their options to remain productively engaged in retirement. After all of those years of hard work an extended period of leisure seemed to be a just reward.

How do they spend their time? A recent survey showed how current retirees spend a typical day:

- 9.5 hours sleep and personal care
- 1.4 hours eating/drinking
- 2.2 hours household activities
- 1.0 hours shopping/services
- 4.0 hours watching TV
- 0.5 hours religious/civic
- 0.5 hours taking care of family members
- 0.6 hours socializing
- 2.2 hours other leisure such as computers, sports exercise, reading
- 2.0 hours miscellaneous distractions, chores

Now repeat this 10,000 times. This is the likely number of days you will spend in retirement. With careers completed and children raised, you will need to find something of interest to take up your newly emptied mental bandwidth. You need to discover something that makes you look forward to each day.

In your current hectic working life, a pending period of peace and calm appears quite appealing. However, after the first year or so of retirement you may find yourself fighting boredom. Many retirees begin to realize playing golf or sitting on the porch for thirty years gets old and seems wasteful.

If you are an active achievement-oriented person you may find yourself 5-7 years into retirement facing an 'old-life' crises. This is the cousin of the 'mid-life' crises but doesn't include sport cars and facelifts.

To many new retirees this may seem to be the last chance they have to use their skills to make a contribution. It is like a retirement rush. There is a last-ditch effort to remain intellectually engaged and relevant. For some it is hard to let go of the old and accept their new station in life. Others will see retirement as an evolving life stage requiring them to take on a new role.

In the pursuit of a new life role you will find there are few role models to follow. There just are not that many people in their late 80's and 90's living active vibrant lives. Many of them remain in hiding and are displayed only for the perquisite family celebration. The few who make the news tend to do things like climb Mount Everest or emulate Mother Theresa.

In many ways, society has been conditioned to view retirement like an event or a goal. This makes retirement like marriage. Once the goal is achieved you expect to live happily ever after. In both cases achievement of the goal gets more attention than how to be successful afterwards. The new retirement is a marathon. The race is not over the moment you retire you are just getting started and there are many laps to go.

Take a moment to reflect on the changes you experienced over the last twenty to thirty years. A lot has happened. A lot more will happen over the next couple of decades. This is time for you to think about second careers, accomplishing long delayed personal goals, starting a fun new business or volunteering to support worthy causes.

You will also need to increase your focus on staying healthy to remain active and delay disability. All of those healthy habits you may have put off due to lack of time now have a more immediate impact on your well being. You will want to slow the age curve of decline through physical activity, diet, and intellectual and creative pursuits.

Living longer increases the likelihood of outliving your friends and loved ones. You will need to attend to creating and renewing support networks to avoid isolation. Continuing socialization needs to become a sub theme to your retirement. This is most important for single retirees with few or no children.

Aging in Society

One way to stress-test a system is to overload it. There are nearly 80 million new retirees preparing to jump on the retirement bandwagon. This is 4-5 million new retirees each year. Signs of stress and strain will appear in likely and unlikely places.

New retirees unprepared for the storm will seek out comfort in the old retirement. It will be like they all are jumping aboard a third world jitney. People hang from the sides shouting and gesturing. The tires flatten and the engine groans as it struggles towards the next stop.

More people attempt to board at each stop. Somehow room is made for them. The bus trudges to the ferry stop where its passengers embark for the journey from the working land to the Promised Land.

The ferry queue snakes for as long as the eye can see as more passengers push and shove their way onboard. The ferry lists port then starboard. There is no room to breathe yet more pile on. You elbow and push your way to form some sort of space to handle your personal affairs while wishing you were someplace else.

The massive number of people coupled with longer life expectancies will test the boundaries of society's institutions and norms. What you see today may not be there tomorrow. Transportation, health, housing and social welfare systems will require massive overhauls to serve the needs of the mass migration of coming retirees. Battles with succeeding generations over restructuring costs are bound to occur.

In a youth centered society, you will need to shape those discussions by having something to offer in negotiations. You can imagine the impact of millions of ninety-year-olds cruising around will have on traffic congestion. Or in the check-out lines as you and others fumble through change purses looking for the debit card you were sure you brought. The reminders will frequent and common.

Your day-to-day life will be affected by this abnormally large number of retirees. All of this activity may change your mind on where you live and what you do. Our cities and suburbs were designed for the car. Somehow you will need to shuttle about to see doctors, friends and family.

Older people use more medical services. Lines for health care will increase and the availability of care will decrease as service demands increase faster than the health system can deliver. Costs will rise and rationing is likely. Medicare does not pay full cost today and most likely will not tomorrow. Forty percent of Medicare costs occur in the last few years of life.

You will need to decide if you will age in place or look for new accommodations. New forms of housing continue to be developed to meet the changing needs of an aging population. Today, active living and assisted living are just two forms of alternative housing. More options are bound to be developed during your retirement years.

How society views aging will evolve. The resulting changes are bound to influence many of your decisions. There will be costs and quality-of-life considerations. Being prepared for the retirement storm requires you to be flexible and to be able to anticipate and quickly respond to the changes around you.

Financial Security

Financial security is where your retirement score is kept. Your score reflects your personal decisions and how well you manage the outside forces affecting your income and expenses.

You know you are more financially secure the less you think about it. You think about it less when you feel you have a plan and the knowledge you have the tools to manage change.

To maintain or improve your score requires diligence. You need to protect yourself from forces deteriorating your lifestyle like inflation and health care expenses. In order to maintain your lifestyle when expenses are rising requires you to be able to increase your income.

Most pensions are not inflation protected. Social Security benefits are less likely to increase over time and there is the potential that benefits may be cut for certain retirees. All of this shifts more of the burden to you and to your personal savings to generate the additional income if you are to maintain your lifestyle.

Your personal savings will face the headwinds of increased taxes to support the new medical care plan. Capital gains taxes rose in 2011 and 2012. It is also possible additional taxes may be required to meet the huge budget deficits.

Demographic changes will affect how money is invested and consumed. Your investment plan will need to reflect this and it will need to be more agile and flexible than when you invested during your working years. The overall result of these changes will likely lower the amount of money you can expect to earn and keep from your savings.

You may face the vice grip of rising expenses and fixed or declining income. Over time, if left unattended, the slow deterioration to your lifestyle from the tightening vice grip may become irreversible.

Up to now, most of your planning for retirement likely has been long term planning. That is, targeting a distant goal and working to achieve it. But, quicker and more frequent change lessens the value of long-term planning and shifts emphasis to short term planning.

In a short term, quicker changing environment you need to focus more attention on management and control of quality-of-life issues and their impact on your income and expenses. You will need to review your personal goals, budgets and investments more frequently. You will need some type of trigger or warning system to let you know when things get sidetracked.

To navigate the storm and manage your affairs in the new environment afterwards you need the ability to anticipate and respond to changes quickly if you are to stay on course. During retirement more responsibility for personal care and financial security will be shifted to you, the individual. It will become more noticeable the longer you are retired.

The farther you move into retirement, the less likely your employment skills will retain value. At some point, going back to work is no longer an option. Lacking the option to return to work will increase the importance of managing all of the elements of your retirement.

The expected shift in responsibility coupled with the need to manage your retirement for many years requires you to learn new skills, tools and techniques. Many surveys show those nearing retirement to be afraid of outliving their money or being unprepared for the many years in retirement. Much of this fear is based on not knowing how to identify and manage the subtle forces affecting their personal and financial well being.

To improve your financial security score requires you to review your personal goals, income, expenses and asset values on a regular basis. The score changes as the game plays out. You will need to make periodic adjustments to keep the score in your favor.

You don't need to spend a lot of time to manage these things. The time you spend on your retirement matters is the financial equivalent of performing maintenance around your house or visiting the doctor and dentist for check ups. It may not be the most fun thing to do, but afterwards you will be glad you did.

But, to do this effectively you need to follow a systematic process to plan, manage and control your retirement. The systematic process presented in the rest of this book will help neutralize the caustic affect of free-floating worries. Learning and setting up the system takes a little time, however, once you learn the system keeping it going becomes a routine that will keep you comfortably in charge.

YOU ARE IN CHARGE

The retirement storm will be disorienting. Surviving the storm will be like traveling to a foreign country for the first time. You don't fully understand the customs, rules and etiquette. You aren't sure how much the trip will cost. You're confused by the language and have difficulty understanding the currency. You're afraid of heading off in the wrong direction and certainly do not want to get sick. Everything is familiar yet different.

When you take a trip a foreign country you make some preparations. You attempt to get an understanding of the culture and society's rules and expectations. You establish a budget to keep spending from getting out of control. You monitor your expenses and have alternate backup plans should things go awry. You check on legal requirements and the availability of health care. With your plan in place, you can relax yet be attentive and enjoy the experience.

So too with retirement, although the trip through the storm and its aftermath is not as well defined. Confusion seeps from the financial service industry and the media often offering conflicting advice or advice too general to be of use. You can't quite get a handle on what to expect and what you should do.

For example, the media encourages you to save more. Generally, this is a good thing. However, when they banter about the need to save something like $500,000, a $1 million, or more the side effect is discouragement and leaves many with a quiet resignation that they will never retire.

Using any target number by itself is misleading. Remember, you need to balance your expenses and income. For example, if you need an additional $1,000 a month from your savings then $1 million of savings is substantially more than you need. But if you need $10,000 a month it is not enough.

Retirement planning as currently practiced is like using a shotgun for target practice. When your goal is twenty years off, loose approximations can be an effective guide. If you veer off plan you have time to make corrections.

The closer you get to retirement or when you are actually retired the more you feel the effects of deviations from this loose general approach to retirement planning. It's like the difference of reading the foreign country guidebook and being on the ground. Your focus needs to narrow.

Retirement planning often gets turned upside down. This happens when the financial component drives the life component of the plan. Instead, your desires on how you want to live your life should be the driver of your plan with the financial component being the reality test.

The question needs to change from this is how much money you have what can you do with it to this is what you want to do how can you do it with the money you have.

Someone needs to take charge of the overall process, and that someone is you. You have the most at stake. It is your life and you live with the consequences. But, in order for you to take charge, you need a system and process to plan, manage and control your retirement.

It is time to look for alternative transportation to boarding the jitney and ferry. With a severe weather pattern approaching it is time to anticipate likely change and make preparations for it. Some may wait for the retirement fairy to save the day but those who choose to succeed plan.

Your experience in retirement will be vastly different than previous generations. You will face a changing, malleable, protean retirement. It will be a retirement where you hold more responsibility for your well being.

To meet this new responsibility, you will need to gain a greater degree of control over the elements defining your quality-of-life in order to succeed. This requires a systematic process to objectively measure and monitor what currently is happening to prepare you for what will most likely happen.

Chapter 2

PREPARATION

When you get near retirement you will need to make a bunch of decisions. You may have to rollover your 401(k), consolidate IRAs, determine pension and Social Security distributions and choose medical insurance options. You may shift your investments to start paying income.

But, beware of the trap many new retirees fall into. Too often they think attention to the minutiae and administrative tasks along with a shift in investment strategy serves as a substitute for true retirement planning. They make these decisions and they think if they know today's income and expense they can manage the rest of their retirement.

In most cases the extent of their management tools consists of an investment statement and a checking account. They tend to keep retirement management in their head. This can work for a few years. Until things get more complex.

Over time inflation slowly erodes their purchasing power. Their savings dwindle and their health deteriorates driving up lifestyle costs. They end up in a weakened position less able to deal with the next unexpected shock.

They become the proverbial frog in the soup pot. The frog is unaware of the water temperature slowly rising until it is too late. Then the frog becomes the soup.

Recent surveys show the majority of prospective retirees' fear running out of money and not being prepared for the retirement long haul. Yet they do little to prepare. Intuitively they know there are a number of forces at work but tend to get stuck solely on their level of savings. To begin you need a sense of what you want to do then the other issues fall into line.

During the thirty to forty years of work you lived within your means; at least on average. What was once novel became routine. Your choice of career and whether or not to have a family were primary factors in how much money you made and spent. The money you made served as a budget which in turn constrained your lifestyle.

Over time career, personal choices and family became ingrained in your every day life. Their conscious influence on money matters faded into the background but influenced everything. Moving from the working state to the retirement state frees up the time and energy committed to career and family leaving a void.

How do you transition this void? How do you seamlessly transform from your working self to your retired self? How do you bridge your retirement experience to your retirement vision?

You may have a picture of retirement in your mind, or you may have a to-do list or just some semblance of what you will do in retirement. Your picture, or vision, of how you see retirement playing out becomes the screenplay for which you seek funding. In the process, you will find your available resources self-edit your vision. Although you still need to live within your means the corollary is to enjoy life and thrive.

Your vision provides the impetus to avoid becoming a sixty-year-old version of a twenty something slacker. It becomes a work in process but is the ultimate driver of your journey through retirement.

The new retirement requires a new way of thinking about retirement. The new retirement requires more than a series of discreet decisions that seem nothing more than following a trail of breadcrumbs. When you pick your head up, you are not sure where you are.

The new retirement requires a new perspective, a new conceptual framework to corral the disparate elements of retirement. You may have seen poles by the side of rivers to help the locals get a sense of a rising river. The poles also let them know where the river is relative to flood stage. This is helpful information.

In retirement, it is hard to notice if your position is slowly deteriorating or improving if you have no means of measurement. Your measurement doesn't make sense unless you know where you are when you take the measurement.

The new thinking for the new retirement starts with your view of retirement, your overall plan. It then brings in various forms of measurements and a process to evaluate the measurements to tell you if your situation is deteriorating or improving while there is time to do something about it. This information is then fed back into the process to help you update your plan.

The new thinking introduces the Longlifer System. The system helps you plan, check measurements, make adaptations, implement changes, review your position and update your plan. It is an ongoing process that keeps you continually aware of your position. It takes a bit of effort to put into place but once set up it is relatively easy to maintain.

This chapter provides an overview of the Longlifer System. The remainder of the book helps you create your version of the system.

At first what follows may seem complex, but most new things are. It becomes simpler as you gain familiarity. Once you begin to understand and master the key concepts, you will increase your sense of control over your retirement.

The Longlifer System helps you prepare for the storm. The better prepared you are the more secure you will be. The system helps you to organize, connect and manage the interactions of the key retirement elements in four steps:

1. Define your desired lifestyle
1. Set guidelines and benchmarks
2. Measure and monitor result
3. Plan, manage and control your retirement

LIFESTYLE

It usually is best to start with the fundamentals. Although striving for well being seems to be an obvious goal, many times retirees seem to lose this connection in times of stress and disruption. To be able to connect current things happening in your life to your sense of well being provides the context to make better decisions.

The better you can connect change and future events to your sense of well being the greater your ability to maintain your lifestyle. This connection provides the intuitive guidance, your radar, to keep you on track.

Your quality of life is reflected by your sense of well being. The medical community identifies key components where present add to the quality of life. The key quality-of-life indicators include:

- Personal well-being. Good mental health, happiness, dignity, healthy appearance, love, knowledge, serenity, joyfulness, and aesthetics.
- Physical well-being. Energy, function, sexuality, mobility, rest, activity and strength.
- Social well-being. Family, friends, support network, connectedness, contribution to others.
- Financial well-being. Financial security, material comfort, independence, confidence in income sources.
- Purposeful well-being. Productive aging, philanthropy, creativity, spirituality, accomplishments and sense of control.

The quality-of-life indicators are the center your plan, your home base. Keeping this a conscious part of your plan provides you a way to get back to the basics when things get hectic.

You probably have heard of sports teams in the middle of a losing streak get a pep talk from the manager to re-focus on the fundamentals. In baseball it's running out grounders, taking the extra base or not swinging at bad pitches. In football it is tackling and blocking.

During your long stint in retirement, you are bound to confront adversity, emotional trauma and financial challenges. In the whirlwind of unexpected change, being able to anchor yourself to the components of your well being keeps you oriented and helps you make intelligent decisions.

Once you set the important parts of your well being, you can measure the level of progress on whether you are enhancing or deteriorating your quality of life. But, the well-being indicators need to be more than absolute measures.

What the measurements do not tell you is if you are enhancing enough or deteriorating the least. This is like swimming at sea. You know you are moving. You are putting in the effort. But what you may not know is if you are making progress or just swimming against the tide.

How long you can retain your pleasant picture of retirement before reality bleeds its edges depends on your level of well being. The more secure you are in the five elements of well-being; personal, social, financial, physical and purposeful, the brighter and more sustainable your picture. The less secure the quicker your picture fades to worry.

GUIDELINES AND BENCHMARKS

This leads us to the second step. You need to define desired results so you can compare what has happened to what you expected to happen to see if you are better off or worse off. You are familiar with some measurements like budgets and rates of return on your savings. When you compare what actually happened to what was planned you know if you spent more than you should have or if you earned more than you expected.

But, to truly make sense of the state of your lifestyle you also need something to serve as a longer-term guide than a monthly or yearly budget. You need something that compares where you are to where you want to be. This is where your vision of retirement takes hold. Your vision helps you set goals and objectives. Once set, these can be measured by intermittent milestones to see if you are on track and going in the right direction.

For goals and objectives to be effective they need to be hatched within the context of something bigger. Otherwise, you end up setting short term goals which may or may not get accomplished only to be replaced by another set of short-term goals. You may have the goal to bicycle through the Provence. Once completed you enter the state of 'now what'.

Goals and objectives tend to be discrete, isolated events. To navigate through the Retirement Storm, you need something to serve as a compass, a beacon, something to guide you through the many years in retirement. You can do this by defining your ideal retirement.

Defining your ideal retirement provides you with direction and guiding benchmarks to determine if you are going off track or moving in the right direction. Defining your ideal retirement may seem at worst like folly, at best an impractical exercise. But, there are some overarching high level ideals common to all of us that can help you get started.

From 40,000 feet people are quite similar. Differences are not noticed until you zoom in and take a closer look. The 40,000-foot view of retirement offers the ability to define high level ideals. The embodiment of these ideals filtered through your personal experiences and preferences becomes your idyllic guide.

The concept of a Longlifer can be that guide. Longlifers have sense of purpose. They are mentally curious and alert. They live healthy lifestyles and work diligently to defer disability. They are financially responsible. They develop and expand on the creative part of themselves to foster expression and communication. They connect emotionally to love ones and their social network. Above all, Longlifers live a dignified life and seek purpose and significance.

If you ever worked in an organization you have encountered policies and procedures that are to be followed when circumstances are outside the routine. The policies and procedures let you know what the organization holds important and what it values.

Similarly, you filter the Longlifer ideal with what you value and what you hold important. It captures your morals, values and priorities. It specifies your long-term self- interest. It reminds you there is more to retirement than scrambling for some extra cash to pay your monthly bills.

You can use the Longlifer ideal as your second set of measurements. It measures relative progress and guides you from the 40,000-foot view to zoom in on and develop your personalized plan. You now have your planned and ideal outcomes that can be compared to what actually happens. These are the cornerstones of your plan.

You define your personal Longlifer guide. This provides you with the structure and context to guide your decision making to steer you to success. Your Longlifer serves as a role model, a target you can emulate or a benchmark from which you redefine your retired self. It becomes the standard to reassure you are on the right track and the buoy to reorient you when things knock you off course.

MEASURE AND MONITOR RESULTS

Much of contemporary retirement planning is about planning for retirement and not actual retirement management and control. You may have a plan, but once you retire it is like being blindfolded as you ski downhill. You have momentum but you do not know where the trees and boulders are or where the slope steepens or flattens.

Too often people create a retirement plan only to set the plan aside and go about their business retaining just the general direction of the plan. In most cases there are too many variables and too many things flying about to strategize and develop a realistic, workable plan that can be put into action. When things get too complicated the human mind strives for simplicity.

Sometimes simplicity has its drawbacks. Many people do not plan or plan simplistically with just a general sense of their monthly budget and how much income they expect. They try to keep the two in balance. But, day-to-day events over time seem to keep tilting them off balance.

Once tilted their attempt to rebalance becomes an over reaction and they move too much in one direction then overcompensate by moving too much in the other direction. Not unlike a car with bad steering and a flat tire it is hard to keep moving forward.

With a paycheck no longer available, you are now are working without a net. The consequences of bad decisions strike deeper and are slower to heal. The more you play pin ball retirement the easier it is to lose track of where you want to go.

I come across many clients who tired of pinball retirement. A typical experience is illustrated by a couple whom I shall call Tom and Debra. Tom and Debra feel they need $3,000 a month to meet their living expenses. Their pensions and Social Security cover most of this with the remaining $1,000 a month to come from savings.

On further inspection, the $3,000 a month is not really $3,000 per month. They forgot to include their quarterly estimated income tax payments now required since there are no payroll withholdings. Also, their monthly budget does not include annual payments like property taxes and auto and home insurance. And by the way, there is that trip and all of the gifts for the grandchildren. It appears $5,000 a month has become their new $3,000.

It is important for Tom and Debra to maintain the appearance of their lifestyle so they take the additional money from their savings to cover these extra expenses in their first year in retirement. Things are bound to get better they think. This is the first tilt.

In the meantime, since they have taken money out of their savings interest rates dropped and their savings portfolio declined in value. This makes it harder for them to continue to take out the additional money from their savings and to have enough left to make ends meet in the years ahead.

They consider taking more risk with their savings to have the possibility of earning a higher rate of return to get back the extra money they took out. This is the second tilt.

Tom and Debra feel they can get through the next couple of years, but are unsure how these decisions will affect the rest of their lives. They contemplate cutting back and lowering their lifestyle. This is the third tilt. As they tilt, waddle and roll through retirement they never quite get the hang of it.

The third step is to measure and monitor what is happening and what has happened. To do this you must organize the various elements of retirement into a conceptually sound framework. There are four broad guideposts that set the framework. They are:

- Personal
- Others
- Income
- Savings

Personal captures all the things you personally want to do and drives your plan. This is where you focus on you separate from your connections to others. What is it that will make you happy? What else do you want to do with your life and so on? The Personal category sets up both financial and non-financial measuring points.

Others measure your relationships with people and organizations. What are the things you want to do with your spouse or life partner? How do you see your relationship with your children or other loved ones? Will you maintain a network of friends and acquaintances? In some cases, your relationships may cost money like collective hobbies, travel and charity work. Others also measures non-financial activities like visiting with your children or playing chess in the park and reflect your overall social goals.

Income is the connective tissue between your lifestyle and your wealth. Your lifestyle needs income to sustain itself. You target the income you need and the income you can generate and work to keep them in balance. Shortages indicate potential problems. Surpluses offer opportunities.

Savings represent your accumulated store of asset value. This includes money flows like Social Security, pensions and annuities which are just different forms of your savings. It also represents stocks, bonds, mutual funds, CDs, investment real estate, and business interests and so on. The value of your savings reflects the ability to generate income and the long-term viability of your plan.

You can view these four categories as a socket and plug. The socket represents the potential juice from your Income and Savings. The plug is your Personal and Other needs drawing out the juice. The connection of the two captures the state of your retirement and serves as one measurement of your overall well being. Is your bulb shining brightly or is it dim and subject to brown outs?

However, your bulb shines, it is critical to get a heads up before you blow a fuse or the power goes out. Things rarely work according to plan so you need a warning system to sound the alarm when your attention is required to a matter at hand. This can be done by determining your range of comfort in each of the four categories.

To measure whether you are straying from your comfort level each category has a Contentment Range. The Contentment Range provides a stabilizing base to each planning area. Once your plan is put into action your Contentment Range serves as the guardrails to warn you when you veer into danger.

Personal Contentment Range

Your budget or how you spend money is the financial part of the Personal area. If you need $3,000 a month to support your lifestyle, you may create a range of expenditures from $2,000 - $4,000. Spending out of this range may require corrective action.

For example, your plan should warn you if you experience three consecutive months where you spent $5,000. You need to understand what has caused the increase in spending. It may temporary and no action is required, or you may need to make substantial adjustments in your daily life.

Spending too little is less of a problem but it could reflect missing payments that could have other repercussion. Or it could reflect a lower cost lifestyle that requires you modify your overall plan.

Your routines, sense of self, health status and your overall expectations make up the non-financial part of the Personal area. Disruptions to any of these can cause agitation and frustration.

Changes around you could interrupt your routines. For example, new aches and pains or a decline in your health status may change the way you approach your daily life. When things change your daily life, you need to have some measurement or reminder in your plan to let you let you know when action is required and your overall plan needs modification.

Others Contentment Range

Currently, your parents may still be alive and in need of your help. Your children may still place demands on your time. You may be working and have connections with your coworkers. At times you wonder how long you can keep this frenetic pace. You seem to always be around someone and feel you have little time for your self.

Your Contentment Range with others is defined by those you keep around you and who you make part of your life. These are the people adding pixels to your retirement picture. They are part of your social activities and provide companionship. These are the people who help you feel safe and happy.

The financial part of the Others' area captures the money you want to spend to support your social life. It makes up the second part of the overall cost of your lifestyle and completes your retirement budget.

The non-financial part specifies your social goals like getting out of the house three times a week or joining the church choir. It captures the activities you want to do with others. Your plan should have reminders to let you know when you are not participating in these outside activities and help you confront the reasons why in order to avoid isolation.

One of the implications of being a Longlifer is that your family and friends may not be Longlifers. You may outlive your spouse, siblings and friends. Your current social network will change and you need to be able to change with it. Over time, your social network will need to be renewed and your Contentment Range readjusted.

Income Contentment Range

The income you need is one measure of your emotional connection to your wealth. The Personal and Others categories identify the money going out, the money being spent. Income represents the money coming in, the income you can generate from your savings. Your Income Contentment Range shows the state of balance between the money coming in and the money going out.

Once you get an idea of how much it costs you to live, you can look to your sources of income to see if your lifestyle is sustainable. You begin by subtracting the amount of money you will get from Social Security, pensions, annuities and other fixed income from your monthly expenses. This lets you know how much you need to take from your savings.

Your Income Contentment Range is the spread around the amount of money you need to take from your savings. For example, if you need to take $2,000 a month from your savings, your Contentment Range may be $1,000 - $3,000. If the amount you are taking from your savings lies outside the range this implies things are out of balance and require attention.

If you find $1,000 a month sustains your lifestyle but you take out $2,000 per month you may be paying unnecessary income taxes. It also could lead growing cash balance that should be reinvested for higher returns.

If you need to take more out of your savings than you planned, then you will have to sell investments where you may incur a loss or a taxable gain. Either way, you will be depleting your principal and you need to know this is going on.

Your Income Contentment Range connects your savings to your lifestyle. When you are outside the range it helps point you in the right direction by letting you know if you are spending too much or your savings are not earning enough. When you are in balance things are fine, if not attention is required.

Savings Contentment Range

Nowhere is your retirement vulnerability more exposed than in the management of your money. You need to trust the system, test the advice of others, know your limitations and have the temperament to tolerate volatility.

Your Savings Contentment Range is the value of all of your assets. The value range of your assets, a floor and ceiling, is where you feel secure. For example, you may feel secure and content when your wealth is between $300,000 and $400,000.

If the value of your assets rises above your Contentment Zone you feel more secure. While a drop below the Contentment Zone feels threatening. Your plan needs to monitor and measure changes in your assets values frequently enough so you can take advantage of opportunities and avoid pitfalls.

Your savings category is the most volatile of the four retirement categories. Outside trends and forces coupled with your investment decisions make for ever changing values. It is easy for you to be knocked out of your Contentment Range for short periods of time. The challenge becomes knowing if being outside the range is temporary or an indicator of what lies ahead.

Retirement Web

Personal, Others, Income and Savings are separate categories yet they interact. Their interaction can be viewed as your Retirement Web. Your web captures the linkages among the areas. When something happens in one category it could reverberate across your retirement web shaking the other categories. The linkages have some degree of cause and effect. If you are aware of the linkages you can plan for the downstream effects

For example, imagine you suffer a health setback that keeps you bed ridden for weeks. You will likely incur expenses beyond what health insurance covers. This money will need to come from somewhere either by reducing other expenses, thus impacting your hobbies, entertainment or other such lifestyle activities. Or, it can come from your savings thereby lowering your principal and its ability to generate future income.

Being bed ridden may also affect your social life, exercise regimen and probably your overall demeanor. When you are aware of the interconnections you can make well-informed decisions on how best to deal with this temporary setback. You have options and choices.

The four categories help you to organize the key elements of your retirement. Through them you can define what is important to you and what you require to remain secure. Knowing the interconnections of the areas helps you to make better decisions and respond intelligently to change.

But the categories and their linkages are just a snapshot of your retirement. By itself it represents a static approach to retirement. For you to have a truly effective plan you need to put it into motion. You need to convert your snapshot to video format.

Plan, Manage and Control Your Retirement

Your actual experiences will differ from what you planned. You need the capability to measure and monitor those differences. The differences then need to be evaluated for you to figure out their impact on your life. Once you see the impact of these changes you can react as needed and modify your plan going forward.

You can gain firmer control over your retirement by creating a model that represents it. You probably have seen a model of a real estate development. You can see the buildings, pathways and parks. When you look at the model you get a sense of how the different parts connect and how the development should end up.

Similarly, you have seen model airplanes, cars and dollhouses. Each represents the actual thing. By looking at the model, you see how things connect and move. The model gives you a firmer grasp of what the real thing is more so than looking at schematics, blueprints and assembly instructions.

Of course, retirement itself is an abstraction. You do not end up with some tangible thing you hold in your hand. Mostly, retirement planning is a set of desires, relationships and formulas. But these can be represented by an image which serves as your model to allow you to see and get a sense of how your retirement works.

When you create a model to represent your retirement, you gain perspective. Your model helps you develop an intellectual framework to provide context for your decision making. To help you form a picture in your mind, consider a vehicle, such as a car, as the structure of your model.

You are in the driver's seat taking care of Personal business. Others are in the passenger seats, while Income is the driveshaft turning the wheels and Savings represents your engine.

Longevity Pod

You can evolve this analogy further by creating something I call a Longevity Pod (LPOD). It encapsulates your car with risk management, asset protection and other safety features. The LPOD provides the framework for you to manage change, remain secure and guide you through the Retirement Storm.

The LPOD is a visual mnemonic device that connects your personal, social and financial lives. It provides the means for you to organize, prioritize, and make informed decisions. It gives you the wherewithal to take charge of your retirement years. It helps you respond intelligently to the uncertain and the unexpected as you navigate through the storm and what follows.

The structure uses the Personal, Others, Income and Savings categories to give it form. It is then enhanced with a systematic process to make it operational. Finally, accessories are added to personalize your model.

(Back of LPOD)   (Front of LPOD)

SAVINGS ←----→ INCOME ←----→ OTHERS ←----→ PERSONAL→

Personal – Personal is all about you. It is the Captain's quarters. This is where objectives are set and personal adjustments made during retirement to solidify your physical, creative and intellectual settings.

This section holds the dashboard, steering, brakes and accelerator of your LPOD. Gauges monitor your Years-to-Go (YTG), Dollars-to-Go (DTG) and risk exposure. Warning lights caution you when your spending or savings are off kilter or if you veer too far from your personal objectives.

The steering wheel represents your decision making process that helps you navigate around retirement debris. While the brakes and accelerator adjusts your spending and motivation to help you achieve your goals.

This section also is the GPS and the gyroscope of the LPOD. It helps you to keep your balance and shows you where you need to go. Everything else follows it. Here you decide which activities you will be doing and what type of lifestyle you will live. Decisions made here affect the operations of the rest of the LPOD.

You adjust the risk gauge on your savings and investments to expend or conserve resources. To spend more or less, to take on more or less risk is based on personal choices. This section provides the flexibility to respond intelligently to the unexpected.

Others - Others represent your loved ones and social life. It identifies your support crew the people you want in your passenger cabin to help you live out your retirement drama. You decide who is on board and whether your LPOD is a two-seater, sedan, minivan or RV.

This section sets the stage for companionship. Here you mingle and get feedback and reinforcement for your identity. You define intimacy, your social life and your support network. This section also offers you the opportunity to help others and to build your legacy. It captures your interaction with the outside world.

The decades in retirement can seem very long if you are alone. Here you can prepare for outliving friends and loved ones. In the meantime, the Others' Section allows you to develop deeper connections with the people you care about. Family history and traditions become more pronounced. Efforts made to keep social networks alive and replenished add immeasurably to your quality of life.

There will be things you personally do not want to do. You may lack the time or expertise to manage certain necessary tasks like insurance, investments or taxes. In this case special quarters can be set aside for a professional crew. Your crew may consist of legal, financial and tax people.

It also can include life coaches, doctors, masseuses and personal shoppers. As Captain, you get to decide who is on board and what tasks will be delegated to outsiders while you manage the overall process.

Income - Income is the driveshaft of your LPOD. It connects your lifestyle to your resources. It is the hum and vibe of your daily life. Now is time to discover your inner accountant. While the Personal and Others sections help you to define your new spending habits, Income determines if they are sustainable.

Once you know your spending habits you will know when to hit the accelerator or brakes to respond to the uncertainties ahead. When you push the Personal accelerator to spend more money, screeches, whines and rattles may signal that you are taking too much income. While a smooth burst of power may indicate your resources are sufficient. The warning lights and gauges let you know when you need to do something.

Passive income becomes your lifeblood, the fuel for your LPOD. Work no longer replenishes your income. You become more dependent your money management skills and the ongoing viability of your Social Security, Medicare and pensions to generate the income you need.

Savings- Savings serves as the power source for projecting your LPOD. It generates income, the fuel necessary for a secure life. As the value of your wealth increases, its capacity to produce income increases. Similarly, a decrease in value decreases income potential.

You may have accumulated IRAs, 401(k) s, 403(b) s, and other financial assets along with real estate and business holdings. The management of these assets takes on a new role. They need to be viewed differently as you do not have the twenty or so years of future employment to help you ride out storms. Poor results are felt immediately.

While you worked, the objective to generate income from your investments was secondary to the objective of growing its value. Once retired your objectives change. Now, you need to convert wealth to income as tax efficiently as possible while reducing the risk of loss. Growth is still necessary to counter inflation, but becomes a secondary priority.

The management of wealth is the second key lever, the first being spending management, to achieve control over your journey through retirement. You can change investments when the environment changes or you can make changes to your lifestyle.

If the value of your investments declines too much for comfort, you can reduce your spending. If your expenses become temporarily but necessarily too high you may be able to shift investments to generate more income. Flexibility provides options.

The dollar value of this power source at any given time provides you with the Dollars-to-Go (DTG) or the level of your fuel gauge and how long your money is likely to last. Once you know how much money you have, you can estimate how much income it can generate. This helps you in the challenge to balance your YTG with your DTG.

Measuring what has happened and comparing it to what was planned, both personally and financially, is probably the least practiced exercise in retirement management. Although it is a key element in achieving success very few retirement plans do much more than measure investment performance.

To be successful, you need a process that you regularly follow. This helps you to get the most value from it. The process measures what happened, what you thought would happen and what you would have liked to happen. With this information at hand, you are in control.

POISE Process

Once you retire you set many things in motion. To direct this motion you will need to measure things. To make sense of your measurements you will need to compare your actual measurements to some standard. You do this through evaluation.

The process of evaluating what has happened helps you make necessary adjustments. The POISE process furnishes the fabric that envelopes your LPOD to create a sheltered protected environment.

The POISE process links the critical retirement components together and operates your LPOD:

- ➢ P - Personal
- ➢ O - Others
- ➢ I - Income
- ➢ S - Savings
- ➢ E - Evaluation

Evaluation completes the POISE process. It is your operating system. The process provides the connective tissue binding the four areas of your retirement. Through evaluation you measure what goes on in each area. This gives you the ability to assess the impact of change in one area and see how it echoes across your Retirement Web.

Evaluation displays the monitoring gauges and safety valves of your LPOD to alert you when you go off course or otherwise are headed for trouble. It feeds the fuel gauge, warning lights and service required reminders. The signals are sent to the Captain's quarters for review and action. This converts your static plan to a dynamic plan.

The process, through periodic review of your retirement experience, empowers you to compare your experience with your vision. The process is a way for you to drive your LPOD through the storm, ensure it's operational and through scheduled maintenance stay on course.

Evaluation allows you to calculate actual and relative movement from your starting point and compare it to your desired outcome for each retirement area. There is a separate evaluation for each of the four areas and one for the overall connection among the areas. Through the POISE process you can assess your progress and adjust to a new starting point each year and start the process once again.

Measurement needs to be both actual and relative. Some things might be measured once a year. Mostly, these are works in progress such as whether you actually stuck to your exercise and diet regimen, completed your foreign travel or began to learn a new language. Or whether you actually initiated new social interactions or got out of the house as often as you planned.

Other reviews can be done more frequently. You might compare actual expenses to your budget on a monthly basis. Investment performance can be measured quarterly. The frequency is up to you. But measurements should be frequent enough to provide timely information but not so often that it engulfs all of your waking thoughts.

With actual outcomes assessed, the next step is to compare them to relative outcomes. This is where the idyllic Longlifer comes in. Your transcription of your mental video of the ideal retirement becomes your Longlifer benchmark and is used to compare where you are to where you want to be. This is your vision being compared to your experience.

For example, your Longlifer wants to travel. But you may have had to take on unexpected expenses which push you over budget for the year. Instead, you decide to forego the trip abroad. On the actual side, you stayed within budget on the relative side you did not meet your Longlifer goal of foreign travel.

Relative measurements also help to keep investment performance in perspective. Your goal may be to earn 6% for the year. Your actual earnings may have been 8%; which is good. However, the rest of the world earned 10% for similar investments which is not so good.

Both actual and relative sets of measurements are important, especially since small shortfalls compounded over twenty to thirty years in retirement can have large unforeseen consequences. With those measurements complete, next is to freeze frame interconnections among your retirement areas.

Each area gets wrapped with your desired outcomes but there are cross connections among the guideposts that also require attention. You may find a new passion that requires more income. This can cross into all four retirement areas.

Or your best friend may have to move thus disrupting your social life. These cross connections need to be surfaced so the changes can be reflected in the next starting point of your ongoing plan.

You need a heads-up when you spend too much or if your savings decline too quickly while there still is time to do something about it. You need to know if your health and social habits turn dangerous when they go AWOL from their post.

Your LPOD helps you to set goals, define your desired lifestyle and determine what it will cost to maintain. It helps you to task your savings to provide the necessary income. It reflects your foundation and shows you how to manage the dynamics.

Entering retirement is like training for a sporting competition. You trained well, psyched yourself up, put on your game face and are ready to go. You will not know how effective you are until you play the game. Once the game begins, your deficiencies get exposed, you encounter the elements and compensate and adjust.

Similarly, in retirement you need to find if out if your assumptions hold. You do this by comparing what you experience with what you planned. The differences are highlighted and inform you as to whether you need to take corrective action. Evaluation and measurement separate the focused from the clueless.

Your Retirement Web will experience stressors when uncertain and unexpected things knock you off stride. The POISE process helps you to recalibrate your retirement picture when it loses focus. It helps keep you on plan and to maintain perspective. This perspective helps you to avoid isolated decisions and their unintended consequences.

You are the Captain of your LPOD. You design it. You operate it. You are in charge. This does not mean you need to know every detail. There are people for that. What you do need to know is how the overall system works and to know how to adapt to problems should they arise.

To make this manageable every captain needs a control panel.

Longlifer Dashboard

Should you spend money today or save money for tomorrow? Do you take unnecessary investment risk for gains today only to face a future loss? Do you eat another container of ice cream today and discount clogged arteries and sagging thighs later?

Studies consistently show we value the here and now much more than something in the future even when to do so is irrational. If all considerations are for something in the future, we tend to be rational. But, when we combine the here-and-now with the future, temptation weighs in on the here-and-now.

The collective compounding of all of these today decisions effect what happens to you in the future. When the future arrives, you may wonder why things are not the way you want. This can lead you to make more today decisions in hopes of rectifying your next bout with tomorrow.

The Longlifer Dashboard serves as the executive function of the pre frontal cortex of your retirement brain. Your executive control seeks out information. It prefers simplicity, clarity and factuality.

A lot of things will get thrown at you in retirement. The buzz and swirl of the moment can disorient you and leave you confused as to the next best direction to take. If you do not have a firm sense of where you are and a good sense of direction it is easy to get lost.

As you hunker down through the Retirement Storm you need to pop up and look around occasionally to make sure you stay on course. Your Longlifer Dashboard displays where you are on your course and serves as your early warning system. It brings together the actual and the relative and the idyllic and the real. It calculates the today tradeoffs with tomorrows' outcomes.

LONGLIFER DASHBOARD

PERSONAL   OTHERS

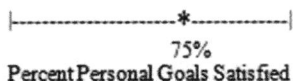   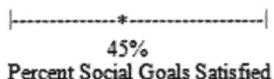

75%   45%
Percent Personal Goals Satisfied   Percent Social Goals Satisfied

INCOME SPENT   SAVINGS

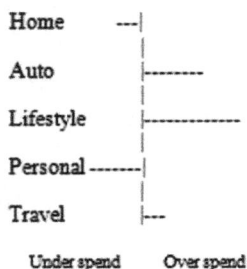   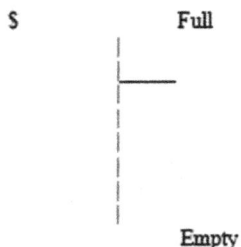

Under spend   Over spend

INCOME GENERATED   TAX EFFICIENCY

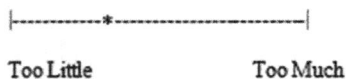   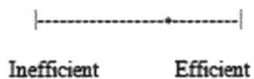

Too Little   Too Much   Inefficient   Efficient

DRAWDOWN RATE   INVESTMENTS

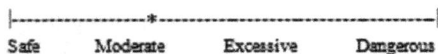   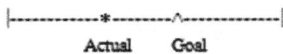

Safe   Moderate   Excessive   Dangerous   Actual   Goal

CHANCE OF RUNNING OUT OF MONEY: 7%

OVERALL RETIREMENT GRADE: 80%   B-

When you drive your car you monitor fuel, engine temperature, oil levels and other critical components to ensure safe travel. So too the elements of a dynamic retirement plan can be collected and monitored. With your dashboard in place, you can see at a glance where work needs to be done and where you are doing well.

If this were your Longlifer Dashboard you would notice certain expenses need to be examined and you need to review your social goals to keep nudging yourself towards your desired lifestyle.

You also are not meeting your investment targets. If your investments are doing less than your target goal, you might call your investment advisor to see what is going on. If you are managing your own money it is time to take a closer look at what you are doing.

Longlifers track these measurements and make adjustments when needed. The dashboard helps provide a level of comfort and a degree of confidence. It measures both the individual guideposts and their cross connections. With measurements in place, you can boldly go forward into retirement.

Building an LPOD may seem like a lot of work. Most things you have never done before seemed daunting at first. Once you have completed a new task it seems it was not so hard after all and once it is done it is simpler to repeat.

This is somewhat like moving. There is the hassle of finding a new place to live and selling your current place. Then you have to pack and physically move then unpack. But, once entrenched in your new abode, life settles itself. After that you keep the house clean and perform periodic maintenance.

Events and circumstances will change your life during your stay in retirement. Once your LPOD is set, periodic maintenance can readily accommodate those changes. This does not have to take much time. Timely reports are readily reviewed. They get calendared like other important things in your life.

During the coming decades you are bound to suffer setbacks and endure painful times. You may feel emotionally overwhelmed by investment losses, health problems and the loss of loved ones. You may get knocked off balance creating doubts about maintaining your security and independence.

As you traverse the Retirement Storm your LPOD provides you with the security and confidence you are doing all you can to ensure a prosperous and joyous retirement. The activities and lifestyle you choose sets the direction. A vibrant social network adds meaning to your life. Income becomes the life source while your savings becomes your fuel source.

You continually measure progress and make corrections where needed. You are in the driver's seat. Your well-being gets connected to your plan and you have the tools to build the bridge connecting your retirement experience with your retirement vision.

The LPOD provides the basic retirement structure. Cars have similar chases, airplanes similar frames and after all a house is nothing but a floor, some walls and a ceiling. Each of these have myriad options as to how they look once completed as does your LPOD. The LPOD provides the structure and context while you provide the personalization. Each design will look different, each will be individualized. Yours will reflect you.

To get started you need the lay of the land in order to know what is likely and what to expect. Now it is time to get on-the-ground intelligence, a scouting report and a GPS to guide you through the Retirement Storm.

Chapter 3

RETIREMENT STAGES

There is an old saying the predicting is hard especially if it is about the future. As a Longlifer you will probably live into your nineties. You will face challenging personal, physical and financial transitions. What these are and when they will occur are somewhat predictable.

The choices you make during these transitions must be decided within the context of the overall changes you most likely will experience. If something is likely to happen in the future, it is helpful to know about it now so you can prepare for it.

Psychologists have been working with human development and identity since at least the 1940s. Initially it centered on children and the various phases of development. Adulthood and maturity were viewed as the last two phases of the human lifecycle. Subsequently, these stages have been further refined. They suggest we face continual development phases throughout our entire lives.

Ongoing development will further refine your identity. You will be need to take a new look at yourself and assess how your identity changes as you age. Understanding how these changes affect you help you transition from a work and parenting identity towards a retired identity.

When you combine your personal development with the physical, social and financial changes retirement brings you can partition likely changes into four distinct stages. These stages create markers to map your destination and make sense of certain things that are likely to happen to you at different times in retirement. The stages let you know what you can expect and provide a relative point for measuring progress as you move through time.

It is hard to give value to something twenty to thirty years out. After all, what is here and now always seems more important. It is easy to adopt the outlook that you will deal with the future when it comes. However, to be financially secure today you must greet the likely events of the future and assign to them their proper recognition. You can facilitate this by separating the future into four stages.

The Stages of Retirement are:
1. Anticipation
2. Activation
3. Consolidation
4. Contemplation.

Each stage has a physical, social, personal development and a financial component that affects your lifestyle and your pocketbook. The age a stage begins and how long it will last vary from person to person.

Longlifers continue to expand their radius of knowledge and experience throughout retirement. They view the stages as rings on a tree. Each ring represents a new year and encompasses all of the previous years. The rings serve to protect and nourish them. They in turn can then protect and nourish those that follow.

ANTICIPATION (3-5 Years Prior to Retirement)

Retired Husband Syndrome (RHS) is a syndrome first identified in Japan. Many older Japanese men's lives revolve around work. They work long hours and after work socialize with each other arriving home late most every night. They wake up the next day and do it again.

Communication with their spouses is not considered their strong point. The stay-at-home wives raise the children, manage the house and when husbands are home, fix their meals. The husband would decide when to retire without consulting his wife, although, he would discuss this with his work buddies.

Once retired and cut off from his longtime office social network, the Japanese husband found he was virtually friendless. He would stay at home, watch TV and bark out orders to his wife. He generally would forbid her from going out with her friends. He lacked the skills to fend for himself and was considerably needy. The typical longevity blessing of Japanese women now became a curse. Divorce was not a financial or social option for the wives.

More and more women developed various physically ailments shortly after their husbands retired. They complained of stomach ulcers, unusual rashes and irritableness. Their doctors found no medical reasons for their ailments and referred them to therapists. Their therapists diagnosed RHS.

Therapists would provide various stress-reducing techniques for the wife and require the husband to modify his behavior. Luckily, there are now over 3,000 support groups nationwide focused on re-educating retired Japanese men to become more communicative and self-supporting. Marriages are healing.

There is more to getting ready for retirement than just saving enough money. You need to prepare the environment for your arrival. Warn the spouse and loved ones. Create an activity agenda. Refine your life management capabilities.

The Activation Stage is the time for this preparation. You need to get an idea of want you want to do, where you want to go and make a clear-headed assessment of where you are today. Uncertainty and doubt at times will linger but they will be interspersed by periods of confidence and bravado.

To prepare for the uncertainty ahead you need to build a foundation that will support your transition from work to leisure. Your life activities, social network, income needs and savings management serve as the four pillars of the foundation and guide you through your preparations.

You can view your retirement as a launch, something that will last a long time. The Activation Stage is the time to prepare your launch as you are at the point of no return. Pilots, astronauts, engineers among others develop checklists to scrutinize and follow diligently prior to embarkation.

This is the time for your to-do list. Certain things need to be done while you still are working like getting a health assessment, paying down debts and maximizing your savings. You will need to review employer benefit options and make decisions on pensions and Social Security.

There will be a list of things you want to do once you retire. This is the time for the big picture. Identify in bold strokes how you see your retirement life playing out. If travel is a goal, list the countries you want to visit. Leave the trip details for later. This is a time to sample the items on your list. Sampling allows you to test whether you like something or not.

Once you determine what you want to do, then you need to figure out who you want to do it with. Much of what you do when you are working centers on your job, networking and social functions that enhance your status in the community. Many of these friends and acquaintances will not be an active part of your retirement.

If you decide to move you will need to build new support groups. Or your to-do list may not coincide with your current friend's to-do lists. This stage is a time to strengthen ties to your loved ones while you begin to build relations with friends who share your retirement interests.

Financially this is the time to estimate the income needed to maintain your new lifestyle. Certain work- related costs, such as commute, clothing and work accessories will decline while other costs related to leisure and your new lifestyle will increase. You need to soberly assess your savings and reduce investment risk.

ACTIVATION (0-10 Years after Retirement)

It may take six to nine months to realize we are not on an extended vacation but actually retired. During this period, you may feel like a snake that just shed its skin or a hard- shelled crab going soft warily eyeing the deep fryer. This period challenges you to let go of the old, embrace the new and evolve.

There are no budget meetings or deadlines. No cranky bosses. No demanding clients. No need to get up early. It is your time on your terms. You worked hard. Now is the time to enjoy the fruits of your labor. You may have used retirement as a motivator to get through work, meet challenges and make sacrifices. Now is the time for payback, to reward your self and to do the stuff of dreams while you work through your to-do list.

You are now one of those slim, trim, active silvered haired people you see in the ads telling you how great it is to be retired. There are pent up desires to satisfy, financial decisions to make and some serious fun to have. Your energy level is high and you may have trouble pacing your self. There seems to be countless things to do.

After some period of time, the frenetic pace slows and you begin to find a new daily rhythm. You become aware you have an abundance of time on your hands. The lack of new accomplishments can gnaw away at you as your sense of importance and accomplishments from your work identity fades. This may leave a sense of emptiness as you feel less needed and doubt shadows your sense of purpose.

Many of the skills and behaviors you learned in your working years provide less traction and garner fewer advantages when you apply them in your new environment. You may have been the boss but now you have to wait your turn in the doctor's office. You cannot order your knees to feel better or cut in front of people during the senior's special lunch buffet. You learn to replace your work skills with the new skills of cooperation and kindness to get what you want.

The Activation Stage is time to transition from self-absorption to generativity. Generativity is caring for the next generation. This can be viewed as transitioning from actor to director, athlete to coach or executive to mentor. This could involve different forms of teaching, showing or guiding. You can teach what you know or learn new things and share them with others.

You begin to realize helping the next generation is in your enlightened self-interest. The next generation can build on the things you did well and learn from your mistakes. They can advance the good things of society.

At some point you find the wishes you make are more for others than for you. You begin to develop the capacity and comfort to give. You can expand your caring circle. Generativity is a form of caring for others. It is a way to begin to let go.

Generativity may or may not add to our YTG, but research studies show it can triple the chances the decade of your 70's is a time of joy. This can be done by teaching and guiding grandchildren, helping those in your community or contributing to the knowledge base for others to share.

Much of Generativity will occur in the Activation Phase of retirement. This is a time to gather with others and have share.

By now the foundation built in the Anticipation Stage has been tested, modified and accepted. You find new dimensions in your relationship with your spouse or life partner that excessive leisure provides. Accommodations have been reached. Goals have been shared or discarded. A mutual understanding carries you forward.

Your new social network once established continues to evolve. You experience mortality flashes as family and friends disappear or become disabled. You hold loved ones closer and listen more attentively to your doctor. If you haven't already learned it you finally get that living healthy is the way to go.

By the end of this stage, you are in full acceptance of your financial position. Lifestyle and budget are defined by your new routines. You know how much you need to live on and you accept the limitations of your wealth. This brings a sense of financial security. Once secure you can focus more on possibilities rather than limitations. There still seems to be a lot for you to do.

By the end of the Activation Stage, your brisk walk-through life becomes a stroll. The to-do list is mostly exhausted. You have a tough time of letting go of the highly active lifestyle over fears you may be giving up. Nevertheless, you do become more attentive to the wonders of everyday life.

CONSOLIDATION (Years 10-20)

There are not a lot of mean grandparents. Most people seem to mellow with age. The assessment of how you lived your life continues to bubble to the surface. The scorecard is in on your parenting. Your children are grown and making their own lives.

You begin to accept the finality of your career accomplishments and shortfalls. The 'would of, should of and could of' reflection eventually resolves itself. You fit better in your skin.

One ongoing challenge will be to avoid stagnation. Stagnation can lead to depression, higher medical expenses and early death. Now, your body seems to have a mind of its own. It tends to rebel more these days. Your activities shift from physically demanding to physically tolerable. Instead of competitive tennis you prefer collaborative fundraising. Relationships and social interaction move up your priority list.

Anthropology shows many societies have elders in the role of 'Keepers of Meaning". All that has come before has been structured into organizations and institutions. The elders maintain these structures and ensure their continuation. They focus on family, social groups, and organizations that fill in the gaps between government and business to add texture to their community.

Caritas, Latin for caring love, is setting aside your self interest for the good of the whole. The Consolidation Stage allows you to make peace with your past and prepares you to take care of others. You learn or have reinforced the joy of giving. Somehow giving seems to make you whole and you become something more than you were. You gain new insights and more fully appreciate things than before.

In your family, it is time to uphold and reinforce traditions. Gatherings offer strength and connectedness to many generations. What has been important for the survival of the family is passed on. Stories satisfy the hunger of younger generations' need to learn of their past and how they fit into the present. They learn from the successes and failures of those who came before them.

Your role changes in your community. You move from the front lines of working with others to working with structures. Instead of actor to director, you are now part of the Academy. Instead of athlete to coach, you now help oversee regional Little League groups. You were working with the homeless now you are on the Boards of Director of non-profits. It is time to step up and widen your radius to create the next protective ring for those around you.

Government takes care of the political, business the economic but you need to take care of the social needs of your community. Around your community are countless non-profits feeding the hungry, accompanying the lonely, cleaning the environment, providing structure for abused children among meeting many other needs.

This is a chance to keep it going. The current volunteers will need to be replaced. There is always a need for leadership, a chance to use your experience and wisdom. There is a need to assume empathetic responsibility for other adults to perpetuate these organizations. Caritas helps fulfill the Consolidation Phase of retirement.

You are now 10-20 years into retirement. There is no going back you only can move forward. You reconsider whether you want to age in place or seek a retirement facility. Health becomes the central focus and its related costs test your financial stability.

CONTEMPLATION 20+ Years

Your contemporaries exchange their cars, clubs and rackets for wheelchairs, walkers and canes. The guys sit in the fiber café swapping scooter stories. While the program director rustles up the white-haired widow wheelchair posse and herds them towards the afternoon's entertainment.

You, as a Longlifer, are on the treadmill in the cyber café adding the finishing touches to your contributions towards improving the habitat of the Madagascar Aye-aye while checking your entry in the Pre-Columbian Fertility Goddess art exhibition.

All of the years of physical and mental exercise pay off. Your bones are strong, muscles flexible and you maintain mobility. You remain curious. Your creativity is your expression. You prepare for the tug-of-war between independence and dependence.

The good old days seem better and past events do not seem so far back. You are focused more on the now and get pleasure and joy from simple things in every day life. Everything, especially people matter more intensely. You want to squeeze and hold meaningful things more closely.

Your inner age catches up to your biological age. Sooner or later the State confiscates your driver's license. Now you rely on that nice young man to take you to your doctor's appointment. Long term planning is lunch next Wednesday. Gradually your life fills up with strangers who make you take pills and tell you what to do. You are referred to by your condition, not your name. The human touch becomes institutional, efficient uncaring.

The familiar fades away. You reconnect with your child-like trust in others but get annoyed when you are treated childlike. Others equate a decline in your physical ability to a decline in your IQ. They don't listen to you, they tolerate you.

Through all of this it is important to maintain your dignity. The Contemplation Stage is about Integrity. It is time to reinforce the integrity of the human experience. We all learn by observation, not just children. We look to see how others handle a particular situation to see if there is something to learn.

The younger generation will observe how you age. They will observe how you deal with the indignities and will seek to be reinforced that the life experience is worth the effort. Aging is not necessarily bad; it is just the next phase of living. You are completing the life cycle.

You find accepting your limitations and the boorish behavior of those around you reduces frustration. Many things that seemed so important seem less so now. The body is in open rebellion. Integrity becomes critical. The wisdom you have gained provides amusement to your observations. You keep your wily wit and press on and your new motto becomes dignity above all.

You learn humility is not a bad thing. Many religious and ancient texts show its purpose. It helps you cope. If you are religious your spiritual experience deepens. If you are more secular you become thankful. Age is a privilege.

It is time to tally up your life score to see what kind of legacy you will leave. There still may be ways of getting extra credit through charitable giving when you go through your life possessions and remaining wealth to decide where it will go.

Your expense pattern becomes dominated by the health care industry and personal service providers. Your challenge becomes giving not getting. You feel you still have so much to share if anyone is willing to listen.

The social network you developed supports you through losses of friends and loved ones. The ties to your family are stronger although they do not visit as often as you like. You get some comfort from them, but in the end it is personal.

Generativity, Caritas and Integrity are ways to put your intent into action. These are terms defined by psychologists to help explain identity and life cycles in the human development. Their theories and studies show aging as a process of development as opposed to one of decay.

For humans, as a species, it seems our primary purposes are to procreate and perpetuate the species. As we age, we may not do much more of the former, but we can do a lot of the latter. We need to support a viable next generation by passing on our knowledge, skills and experience.

We need to ensure social organizations are structurally sound. Finally, as we age, we are still a role model for the younger set. They will look to us on how to age, or worse, how not to age. How we age matters.

Picture an old person sitting on a chair alone. What do you see? Is the person lonely, abandoned? Is the person self content? Is the person vulnerable or secure? You may have had the experience at age 15 or so, on a wonderful summer day with many things to do and notice mom or dad sleeping on the couch. You wonder how they could sleep on such a day with so much to do.

From their perspective, it was the most glorious thing they could think of doing. After a long week of work, chores and other demands, this was their time to luxuriate in a nap. You were the fifteen-year old full of energy, you slept on the couch and you will sit alone on the chair. Your perception of aging influences your behavior.

The Stages of Retirement identify the physical, social, financial and personal transitions you will face. The more effective you are in making the transitions the more gratifying retirement. You move from something you have known for 30-40 years to something you have never done before. Desirable role models are scarce. Guidance is available but you have to find your own path.

The stages are stepping stones in retirement. They lay out possible paths for you to follow. Which path will you take and how you will stay on the path depends on what drives you.

PURPOSE AND THEMES

Studies show a purpose-driven life tends to be a happier and longer life. Purpose gives you a reason to wake up to each morning, something to look forward to. There is a sense of things yet to accomplish, an opportunity to contribute. All of this adds zest to your life.

Some people know exactly what they want. The goal driven will set goals, objectives, timelines and budgets. The curiosity driven will enjoy the journey. They will set a course and let things unfold. The porch dwellers will stop and smell the roses and be in a power down mode for years to come.

Others are not so sure what they want. If you are like most new retirees the future is wide open. Narrowing it to make it useful is hard. You may remember trying to figure out what you wanted to do when you grew up. The choices are many. Mostly, you knew what you didn't want to do. Figuring out what you wanted to do was harder.

What do you want to be when you retire? Getting started is the hardest part. If a strong sense of purpose is eluding you, a fallback option is to create a theme for your retirement. A theme can serve as guardrails to keep you on the right path. It helps you to set a direction and makes clearer what you want. It helps you determine the things you will do in retirement.

Themes in retirement are like themes you may have used to plan a vacation throw a party. For example, once you think of a theme for a party, the rest of the party falls into place. You now know what kind of food and drink to serve, who to invite and how to decorate the place. With this knowledge it becomes easier for you to figure out how much things will cost and how you will pay for them

Themes set the basis for your retirement activities. They provide centeredness, something that can guide you on a daily basis. They help you focus. Your theme should be something you have gravitated towards for most of your life. This is what is important to you. Your theme should reflect what you value and what you want to project into the world. The key retirement themes include:

- Family
- Adventure
- Philanthropy
- Personal growth
- Activism

For example, if your theme is Family you may live near your children and grandchildren. You can teach the next generation the values and attitudes you found necessary for success. You could plan annual visits where you bring in the children and grandchildren. Or you could travel the country visiting your brood.

College funding could be set up for the grandchildren. Family rituals could be reinforced or new ones established. You may develop and reinforce your family tradition and culture. Your social life remains separate but it is secondary to the family life. This begins to help you figure out what you will be doing in your retirement years and makes preparing for it easier

In an Adventure theme you could climb Mt Kilimanjaro, sail the South China Sea or spelunk in Argentina. You could move to some exotic locale. You could study and learn new things. In turn you can share your experiences and teach others who may be interested in this lifestyle. You can volunteer time to non-profits who package adventure trips for the disadvantaged or a younger generation looking to build leadership and confidence.

As you slow done physically, you can begin a blog or create some forum for sharing your experience or teaching others some of the things you learned. Your social life will be dramatically different than when you were working. An Adventure theme is considerably different than the Family theme and it has its own spending pattern.

In the Philanthropic theme you look to your community to see what needs to be done. You might identify something the government and non-profits have overlooked. Or you could affiliate with a non-profit and work the front lines for awhile. Gradually, you could work your way up the organization through marketing, finance or fundraising. You could end up being an active member of the Board.

A Personal Growth theme may find you learning new skills or pursuing a path completely different from your working self. You may have worked in business but now you want to do something creative. Maybe you will go to culinary school or study watercolors. You may become a minor expert on astronomy. You can teach what you learn and join or form organizations with similar interests.

Activism may see you getting involved in local or national politics. Or you may take on global environmental or health issues. You can study to become expert in your chosen area and advocate positions. You can create websites, blogs and other media to get across your message.

Each of the themes allows you opportunities for Generativity, Caritas and Integrity to transition yourself through the stages of retirement. You can develop new skills and over time move from the more physically engaging to the more sedate while staying intellectually and socially active. You can continue to gain a sense of accomplishment and personal value.

Choosing one theme does not exclude the others. You can be family-centered and still travel extensively. You can be adventurous and be an activist. Themes help you set your priorities and serve as reminders as to what is important to you. They help you develop a purpose.

Themes give form and direction to the planning process. It makes it easier for you to figure out how much income is needed and whether you can afford your new lifestyle. It establishes your retirement environment.

Each theme can be separated into centeredness and focus components. Where centeredness is closer to whom you are; focus is more of what you do. Together they determine your day-to-day activities. It fills up your time with things that add meaning to your life and can give you a sense of enthusiasm. These activities create your lifestyle.

Using themes to define your purpose through centeredness and focus helps you to establish your new identity. You are now doing something that is important to you, has meaning and contributes to society as a whole. The following questions may be helpful to identify your theme and get you started:

Centeredness	Focus
* What are you passionate about?	* What do you have left to accomplish?
* What gets you up in the morning?	* What makes you feel good?
* What do you value?	* What do you have left to experience?
* How do you want to be remembered?	* Who do you want to help?
* What is your fondest hope and your greatest fear?	* What do you look forward to?

Try to write your answers down. Explore them for themes. You need to have something to carry you for years not just the first few years of retirement. Some things will be finite others will be lasting. The finite things are milestones and can measure progress. The lasting thing can be built upon and carry you through the Stages of Retirement.

Identity is a work in progress. As it evolves and changes, so will your income need. It is not an exercise done once and considered resolved. It is a critical component of the ongoing retirement process.

Part II

LIFESTYLE

Chapter 4

PERSONAL VISION
STEP 1 - PERSONAL

Your Personal guidepost helps you define the first part of your new lifestyle. It helps you figure out how much money you need to maintain this lifestyle. Yet how much money you will need is not simply how much you currently are spending. You need to figure out how much money you will be spending as opposed to how much you have been spending.

Too many people take their current monthly budget and project it into the future. Doing this constrains opportunities. It acts as blinders and they miss out on what is possible. Over time this constraint makes them feel cheated, as if they have missed out on something important.

The storm will rattle your money house. It will easy for you to be distracted when figuring out how to replace lost income or cover newly imposed expenses. You will need something to anchor you to your priorities

Your Personal guidepost serves as one of those anchors. It helps you to identify what you want to do in retirement. You start with your retirement theme. Your theme sets the perimeter for your plan. It captures the things you want to do.

You may start out with a wish list which is fine. The wish list makes sure you have covered all of the things that are important to you. As you begin to convert your wish list to dollars, you can surgically pare it where necessary.

In later chapters you will be shown how put numbers to your budget, but first you need to get a broad sense of what you plan on doing. This begins with your theme and is supported by doing the things that keep you healthy and defer disability. Being sick and disabled tends to void other activities and creates financial stress.

Longlifers look to the factors that contribute to positive aging. They look to get the odds on their side. They do the things that increase the chances of good things happening and decrease the chances of bad things happening.

At this stage of your life, you have done what you've done. Past lifestyle choices are wired in. Studies show it is not too late. There still is time for you to get the odds on your side and increase your YTG.

One longitudinal study identified many significant findings for positive aging. These characteristics add YTG:

- ➤ 70% of college-educated study members age 60 will be alive at age 80 while 33% of the general population will live to age 80. The connection seems to be college-educated tend to have healthier lifestyles. They smoked less, exercised more, ate better and abused alcohol less.
- ➤ Being surrounded by good people offsets some of the bad things in life.
- ➤ Healing loving relationships aid positive aging.
- ➤ A good marriage at age 50 predicted positive aging at age 80.
- ➤ Alcohol abuse shortens life.
- ➤ Learning to play, intellectual and creative activity, and learning how to make younger friends as you lose older ones adds more to life's enjoyment than money.
- ➤ Good physical health and good subjective health add to successful aging.

The study's findings track the impact of past and current behavior on successful aging. Other studies show adopting positive behaviors at a later age can increase longevity and provide a positive aging experience. It is never too late.

Longlifers know there are no guarantees. They also know it is to their advantage to get the odds on their side. They will do the things shown to add to the quality and length of their lives. They begin with themselves.

You need to maintain a healthy self image as you age. This can be hard to maintain when society's social cues portray people over 70 as being feeble, unhealthy and needy. A 2005 Census Report showed 20% of aged report being clinically depressed at any given time.

Also, there is a correlation between depression and Alzheimer's disease. Inactivity, poor self image and the lack of passion leads to higher medical expenses, a higher probability of needing nursing home care and an overall grumpy disposition.

One key to financial security is staying healthy in mind and body. This is more achievable if you are active doing something you love and something of value. Physical activity, intellectual curiosity, creative activity, a good diet and helping others seem to be the keys to a long vibrant life.

These characteristics need to be a part of your Personal Guidepost.

Physical Activity

You need an exercise room on your LPOD. Studies continually show higher activity levels correlate highly with longer lives. The aging parts of your body work better with use and maintenance. Neglect leads to decay. Longlifers thrive; they spend little time in convalescence and delay disability for as long as possible. This partly accomplished by being active.

A paper published as back in 1997 showed the loss of muscle strength is the limiting factor for an individual's chances of living an independent life, defined as limited disability, until death. Additional studies showed feebleness is not only preventable but can be reversed with exercise. Loss of muscle strength is a major contributor to disability as you get older.

Your brain also benefits from exercise through increased blood flow. This helps you to lower the likelihood of various forms of dementia. It provides greater energy levels and allows you to pursue your interests. Exercise tends to lower blood pressure and keep weight off. It also makes you look and feel younger.

You may have an active physical regimen. It may only need to minor adjustments to incorporate activities specifically designed to help aging. If you have put off exercise for years thinking you will do it later, later has arrived. There is not much later left.

Studies show a combination of various activities work best. It is better to stay continuously active than to run marathons or be a great weekend exercise warrior. You need aerobics, muscle strength, balance and tranquility.

AEROBICS	STRENGTH	BALANCE	TRANQUILITY
Swimming	Resistance Training	Yoga	Meditation
Skating	Weights	Dancing	Hobbies
Treadmill	Jogging	Tai Chi	Massage
Stationary Bike	Real Bike	Ball sports	Faith
Walking	Walking	Walking	Walking

These are just some effective activities. You may add additional ones. The key to successful physical activity is to choose one or more activities that cover each column. and do this activity at least four times a week for a minimum of thirty minutes. You get the major benefits through continuous sustainable exercise instead of short bursts of strenuous exercise. Since you are retired, you no longer can use the lack of time excuse.

Some activities may offer a combination of desired traits such as jogging or dancing. Note there is a difference between running five miles on a treadmill and five miles in your neighborhood. That difference is gravity.

When you run in your neighborhood you encounter inclines and declines and this muscle resistance is not adequately duplicated on treadmills. The resistance from gravity leads to additional muscle strength through jogging as opposed to using the treadmill. Jogging provides both aerobics and strength.

Aerobics is great for improving your body's capacity to process oxygen. This helps your heart and can warn off high blood pressure, depression and other undesirables. It helps you to burn off calories and to maintain weight.

Strength training does more to increase your metabolism than aerobics. It burns more calories and builds more muscle mass. Greater muscle mass in itself will require more metabolism to be maintained and burn more calories in the process.

The additional strength you gain will help strengthen your bones. Stronger muscles and bones will prolong your independent living and lessen the need for walkers, canes and wheelchairs.

Balancing exercises coupled with strength activities help reduce falls. Falls are the leading cause of broken bones and temporary disabilities among older people. These activities increase your flexibility and can ease many daily chores. It makes it easier to tie your shoes.

Recent studies show physical fitness appears to reduce the loss of brain tissue and improve cerebral functioning. Apparently, exercise elevates the levels of a neurotrophic factor which acts to increase the number of synapses, develops new capillaries in the brain and protects neurons against damage. This can delay mental disabilities.

There is a need for quite time. Building in something that provides you with a sense of tranquility helps you to re-energize and keep your priorities straight. You may find tranquility in faith or by spending time in nature. A day at the spa or getting lost in a favorite past time can help you diffuse built up tension. Learning to relax lowers your blood pressure, improves circulation and reduces inflammation.

You may think since you are retired, you have no worries. True, work related issues no longer matter. But, Longlifers will experience loss as loved ones die. Life related tensions will still exist. You will worry about your children and grandchildren. Financial and health concerns will perk up and daily frustrations can build over time. There will continue to be a need to chill.

Many studies conducted on people who live beyond age 100 found they had a belief in a higher power or a sense of letting go of daily turmoil. The key appears to be not to carry the world's burdens on your shoulders but to send this off to something outside your self.

You can use a worry box, a place where you temporarily set aside your worries or a to-do list to free you from feeling overwhelmed.

INTELLECTUAL ACTIVITY

Next to you exercise room, you need an activity center. If you are going to live longer, you need to have something fun to do. As you pack your toys and distractions for the trip through retirement you need to ensure we have something to challenge you intellectually and to allow you to express your self creatively.

To maintain your cognitive ability, you need to use your brain. It shouldn't stop working in retirement. You exercise your body to increase strength and stamina. You also will need to exercise your brain to maintain your mental functioning. Studies show the brain's synapses retain their ability to change. Your brain can become stronger and more effective throughout your life. Studies show this may also be true of nerve cells.

The cells and synapses need excitement otherwise they get bored and whither away. What keeps them excited is varying input. As new stimuli are introduced, they need to make new connections. All of this activity makes them stronger and more resilient. New learning activity creates new electrogenicity. Stronger and more active brains tend to be better at delaying cognitive loss and the onset of various forms of dementia.

When exercising the body, you feel the strain in your muscles and lungs. If you engage in some fun activity like a softball game, you do not notice the strain at the time but you may feel it the next day. Brain exercise is somewhat similar. You can work your brain hard such as memorizing something or you can learn something fun and not notice the effort. In both cases your brain is making new connections.

Studies show learning something new as being the most effective form of brain exercise. If you are mathematically or scientifically skilled you might want to read literature classics while if you are scientifically shy you might want to learn about astronomy. Both can attempt to learn a new language.

There may be lots of things you would like to learn but were unable due to work. You may not have had the time. These can be considered the fun activities. For example, you may find architecture fascinating. You can read books, take a class at the local college and join discussion groups. To further your experience, you can travel to the places where this architecture is prevalent and you need to learn a conversational language.

Mixing and matching learning activities will keep your synapses and neurons excited. They will return the favor by keeping your mind sharp and inquisitive.

CREATIVE ACTIVITY

About twenty years ago a French psychologist had an idea. He felt everyone had some degree of creativity inside them. Tired of experimenting on students, like most psychologists, he decided to test his idea on old people. His contention was everyone had something to say and old people, contrary to society's belief, can be creative.

He began his program at a public hospital for the aged in a suburb of Paris. He invited a group of Parisian painters to work one-on-one with the hospital's patients. A number of studios were set aside in the hospital for the art work. Each participant was given a key to do their work at any time of the day or night.

The professional artists found they could bring out inclinations and emotions many elderly people did not know they had. Most importantly the need to be creative was found in nearly everyone. This created quite a buzz among the previously sedate denizens.

The art allowed for the unique perspective of each patient. This became a form of communication and provided a sense of independence and autonomy. They were able to do this on their own, separate from the care givers. The liberation creativity provided allowed for a personal transformation in their aging.

Creativity comes from the heart and gut. It puts something out in the world that has not been there before. It differs from intellectual activity, which is of the mind. Creativity allows you to express your passions. It can help you communicate in a different way and can liberate trapped feelings.

As you move through the Retirement Stages you will experience a variety of emotional challenges. The people you care about may become disabled or die. You will confront your physical and mental deterioration and ultimately your mortality. The emotional turmoil created by these events needs a way to unwind and to express itself in order for you to come to an understanding and to learn acceptance. Creativity can provide you with emotional resilience.

You may think you can't even draw a straight line, how can be creative. Creativity does doesn't have to be limited to the visual arts. The performing arts offer opportunities in community theatres. Poetry, journals and literature offer avenues to explore your thoughts and tweak your imagination. You may find you enjoy special interests and hobbies like cooking, sewing and gardening each can reflect your creative inklings.

You may resist putting your creative endeavors out there for others to experience. You may hesitate to share your new creative take on meatloaf at the next family potluck. You may want to confine your singing to the shower and recite poetry aloud only when no one is around. This works. The key is to begin the creative process. If on the other hand you like to share, there is a whole world out on the internet.

Like physical activity you need to commit to a regimen of intellectual and creative activities. Below are some activities to get your imagination rolling:

INTELLECTUAL	CREATIVE
Learn a language	Visual, performing and other Arts
Study a new subject	Food
Crossword puzzles	Design
Games	Learn to play an instrument
Learn a new skill; sailing, numerology	Write

Some activities combine intellectual and creative characteristics. Learning to play the piano is both challenging intellectually and allows for creative expression. Intellectual and creativity activity keeps your inside in shape just as physical exercise keeps your outside in shape. Both are important to increase your YTG and help you age successfully.

DIET

Now that you are committed to all of this activity, Longlifers need to maintain their energy level. The LPOD needs a dining room. Recent studies show how an intelligent diet can be important to the aging process.

During World War II Americans' diets were limited. Meat was hard to find and when found tended to be expensive. Sugar and fats were rationed and consequently were rarely found in the daily meals. Families sacrificed and pulled together for the war effort.

After the war, the US found resurgence in its prosperity. Coinciding with this prosperity was the reintroduction of meats, sugars and fats. Partly to make up for the sacrifice and partly due to new affluence, these items became daily necessities and in some way rights, to the new American Diet. Large steaks, baked potatoes smothered with butter and sour cream and decadent deserts became common. Fruits and vegetables were after thoughts.

As life became more hectic there was less time to prepare and cook meals. Processed foods miraculously appeared and you were able to get mega-calories with little effort. During this hectic period your job became physically less demanding and more intellectually challenging. The tendency was for you to use fewer calories while you consumed more.

This became a lifestyle for many of Americans. As with most habits, it was given little thought. They just ate what they liked. Decades of eating a lot of meat, saturated fats, sugar and processed foods led to an obesity crisis, higher incidents of diabetes and chronic lifestyle diseases, and a shortening of life. Similar patterns are starting to be seen in developing countries today.

Education on the dangers to your health from this lifestyle has been ongoing for quite awhile. Diet fads come and go. Scientific studies tell you one day that something is good for you and the next day another study says it is bad for you. The results of these studies are conflicting and confusing.

Most studies focus on one element and develop its hypothesis around it. For example, a number of studies were done to see the health affects of nuts. Nearly all of the studies reported nuts to be a positive for your health. At first there were concerns of the fat content. So, they warned us off nuts.

Later, the fat content was determined to be good fat so now you can consume nuts. But, wait, since there is all of this fat there also are a lot of calories. S, you should not eat too many nuts. A caveat to most of the studies state they thought nuts were good but could not rule out that the nuts simply replaced something bad like the cohorts were eating double bacon cheeseburgers.

The way studies are done, they will never be able to isolate all of the variables affecting health. They cannot truly separate stress, personal biochemistry, attitude and other things separate from diet that alters your health. Now, what is hot today may be cold tomorrow.

To break through the confusion, there seems to be three general categories for healthy eating. Scientific consensus agrees inflammation, oxidation and aging to be the critical factors in determining a healthy diet.

Your digestive tract is the diet scorekeeper. Adult digestive tracts have an average of two hundred square feet of surface area. This is larger than most family rooms. Food travels thirty feet from end to end. It is an amazing system when it works properly. It is loaded with friendly bacteria that aid digestion and food processing.

Meats, sugars, processed and junk foods change the friendly nature of the bacteria to unfriendly. Bacteria behaving badly throughout a surface area of a family room results in inflammation. Angry bacteria are good if we are fighting infection.

But, upsetting them unnecessarily accelerates heart disease, bone loss, aging and Alzheimer's disease among other maladies. Inflammation knocks your immune system off balance and leads to many age-related diseases.

The oxidation process in your system works like rust on metal. It wears out the tissues and organs of your body over time as you breathe you move oxygen into your cells. Through metabolism, unstable oxygen molecules are formed. These are called free radicals. The free radicals agitate nearby molecules in destructive ways.

While the free radicals run amok, the oxidation they cause tightens skin and leads to wrinkles, promotes the build up of plaque in your arteries, increases the inflammation in your joints leading to arthritis, damages the retina in your eyes and increases the risk of certain cancers. It has also been linked to Alzheimer's disease. Oxidation unites aging and disease.

While you befriend digestive bacteria and pacify the free radicals with antioxidants, aging lessens your system's efficiency. Aging is not a disease just the state of affairs. You can compare aging of your body to the aging of a machine. Wear and tear takes its toll but preventative maintenance prolongs functioning. Aging is like a long road that ultimately comes to a dead end. Your challenge is not to take one of the off ramps.

The longer you travel this road the more exposed you are to uncertainty. Here you confront the rolling of the DNA dice and the hazards of life. In old age your immune system is thirty to fifty percent less effective than it was in middle age. You do not process nutrients as effectively and you lose the resilience of your youth in overcoming poor lifestyle choices.

Those things you did in your youth that supposedly reduced your life expectancy by five years or so meant little then but those five years takes on new meaning when you are in your seventies. Aging occurs at the cellular level and your challenge is to slow the process as much as possible.

One impact of aging is the making and storing of vitamin D. Vitamin D is not truly a vitamin but a hormone produced by the action of sunlight on our skin. Aging draws vitamin D out of your bones and into the bloodstream. The lack of vitamin D reduces muscle strength and bone density.

This leads to brittle bones and weakening of key hip and leg muscles. The chance of falling and breaking bones increases substantially. This reduces your mobility and independence and increases your medical costs. Also, there is a strong link between broken hips and the shortening of life.

Your body's ability to make and process other vitamins also lessens. Mostly this leads to reducing the effectiveness of your immune system. A weakened immune system makes you more susceptible to disease.

Diet plays a critical role in setting the speed of aging. A good diet slows the aging process and helps you from the inside out. A poor diet accelerates aging and tends to force you onto one of the off ramps well before the end of the road. You have been hearing this drumbeat for a while, but bad food intake corrodes the body's engine. This leads to malfunctions like disability and early death.

Studies confirm much of the old wisdom is pertinent today. Everything in moderation. Add variety to your food intake, eat lots of fruit and vegetables and limit meat and fats.

The Mediterranean diet does this. It consumes fruits and vegetables in a variety of shapes and colors; uses olive oil as a primary fat, beans and legumes as primary protein sources, limits meat and processed foods and adds a couple of glasses of wine to add conviviality.

The Asian diet also is based on a variety of fruits and vegetables, uses sesame seed and peanut oil as primary fat, and soybean and tofu as primary protein sources supplemented with fish.

The American vegetarian diet is somewhat similar to the Mediterranean diet but without the meat and it limits dairy products. Overall, the studies show changing your diet later in life still has a powerful positive affect for you to live long and delay disability.

Now you can finish the personalization of the forward part of your LPOD. You need to take care of your self first. From this point-of-strength you can interact and help others. It takes vision, work, fun and sensibility.

Your LPOD will have a contemplation room, an exercise room, an activity center and a dining room. You personalize the rooms. Here you express your personality, desires and traits.

Your activity room may have a large screen TV with the latest WII exercise 3d programs. Or it could have an easel and a palette of paints. Dinner may be pasta fagiolli or tofu and raw vegetables. You may golf or run or do yoga.

The Personal guidepost is the first step in defining your lifestyle. Below is a sample profile you can use to begin the process.

SAMPLE LONGLIFER PERSONAL PROFILE

Categories	Short Term Plan	Longlifer/Ideal
Primary Theme		
Family	Annual holiday gathering	Build tradition
	Visit out-of-town kids	College funding
	Take grandkids on trip	90th birthday party
Secondary Theme		
Adventure	Take 2 trips	Explore Asia & Africa
	Backpack Rockies	Create travel website
	Learn to sail	85th birthday abroad
	Winter in warmth	
Physical Well Being		
	Walk everyday	10 mile walk
	Golf	10 handicap
	Tennis 2 x week	Win club championship
	Practice faith	Lower blood pressure
Intellectual Well Being		
	Mandarin level 1	Mandarin Fluency
	Learn backgammon	Ranked backgammon master
	Study astronomy	Create astronomy club
Creative Well Being		
	Study acting	Role in community theatre
	Sketch	Convert bedroom to studio
	Learn guitar	Play at 90th birthday party
Diet:	Mediterranean	Lower cholesterol
	Gardening	Lose 10 pounds

Longlifers do the things necessary to increase the odds of living long and thriving. Their theme guides them. They develop a retirement identity, add physical, intellectual and creative activities that are supported by a healthy diet. With all of this fun and activity, you need someone to share it with. It is now time to choose the passengers and crew on your LPOD.

Chapter 5

SOCIAL LIFE
STEP 2 - OTHERS

Purpose is rarely fulfilled alone. Legacy is unattainable in isolation. Interaction with others adds texture and meaning to the fabric of life. Others provide a reflection of your self and give you dignity and respect for the life you live. We all need to love and be loved as we search for meaning and significance.

A 2005 Census survey showed over twenty percent of the aged are clinically depressed. Another study shows in 2000 nearly 10 million people over age 65 lived alone. This number is expected to climb to nearly 13 million people by 2012.

Research shows social isolation has a similar effect on your health as high blood pressure, obesity, lack of exercise or smoking for illness and early death. The socially isolated are seven times more likely to be alcohol dependent, four times as likely to smoke heavily and twice as likely to exercise little or not at all.

These all are precursors to a shorter life and one filled with medical complications and higher medical expenses. The socially isolated are more prone to disability and more likely to enter nursing homes. Those who are isolated and feel alone are two to three times more likely to die over a given period versus similar people who have social contacts.

You will need companionship and help to survive the storm. Once you get through the storm you and those you care about will need to do some level of rebuilding or restructuring to reflect the new reality. You will need to support others and get support from others.

Social support is a critical marker in longevity. Your LPOD needs an entertaining and greeting room to next to your Personal quarters. Look around at your family and friends near your age or older. As a Longlifer, the odds are you will outlive most if not all of them. Although those specific relationships can't be replaced, you will need to create an environment where you can continually evolve your relationships.

Through the Activation Stage, or the early years of retirement, you will transition from work related social connections to your retired social connections. The early years of retirement are like summer break from school. The euphoria of all of this new found free time wears off after a while. The Wednesday Bowl-a-Rama with your coworkers needs to be replaced with other social activities.

Your need for meaningful relationships will affect where you choose to live and the types of people you choose to spend your time with. Once retired, you will need to take relationships to the next step to create a socially interactive environment. Now is the time to carefully build your support structure to prevent you from becoming isolated in later years.

While creating your support structure, you need to be careful who not to hang out with. You influence and are influenced by those with whom you spend time. A 2007 medical study showed people who associate with overweight people tend to become overweight. Although this will allow you to blame your friends for being fat you still will need to lose weight.

Follow-up studies showed similar results with groups of depressed people and people with negative attitudes. The longer you associate with such groups, the more likely you are to adapt to group behavior.

Living to 100

There is a lot of research on aging going on today. The scientific community is looking for ways to help us learn the critical elements of successful aging. One area has been to study those living to age 100. Researchers are hoping they can discover secrets or attributes helpful to us all.

They found numerous pockets of people breaking the century mark living in different parts of the world. The groups were primarily located in Southern Europe, Southwest US, Central America, and Asia. They looked at the habitat and behaviors to see if there were common traits linked to living a long life.

They found a number of individual traits deemed to be helpful in each group but those common to all are:

1. Valued Life Role
2. Diet/Exercise
3. External Control
4. Companionship

The first three attributes were covered in the last chapter and are things you can do alone or with others. The fourth requires other people. Those living beyond age 100 integrated these attributes into their lives.

Each geographical area reported the importance of being valued and contributing something of value to those around them. The 100 year- olds defined and found a Life Role to play in their family and community. You can use your retirement themes to help you further define your role.

Their diets were mostly plant based. Animal protein was consumed in small quantities as were saturated fats and high caloric desserts. Soy, nuts and legumes supplemented animal protein. Overall, there calorie intake was low and none were considered overweight. Your focus on preventing inflammation and oxidation will help to slow your age curve.

Their exercise was mostly ongoing movement. Some walked the hills while herding sheep. Others walked to the general store and carried back supplies. Most had vegetable gardens. Although they did not have Pilates and treadmills, they were quite fit. Walking daily seemed to be the most practiced exercise activity. The activities you choose to maintain your physical well being need to be practiced regularly.

Common to the group was the belief in an external locus of control. They were able to let go of things that bothered them. The sense of resignation and acceptance of things around them helped to keep their stress level low.

The religious used faith in God the secular believed in ancestors or others beyond the physical plane to watch over them. You may or may not use faith to help you through stressful times, but to survive the storm, you will need some activity or ritual to help you blow off steam and relax. The tranquility portion of your physical well being activities can help you to cope with stressful times.

The fourth attribute is companionship. None of the 100 year-olds were alone or in nursing homes. They each had strong connections to family and friends. Most also were connected to their village at large and played an integral role in the life of others.

Successful aging requires others. Your plan needs a conscious component to reflect your need for socialization. Awareness of the importance of social connections can easily get dropped over time as people drift apart and financial concerns move to the forefront of your thinking.

If the storm forces you to make financial cuts in the future you need to be sure your cuts won't lead to loneliness and isolation. Having a separate component for your social life in your plan ensures it receives proper recognition.

Loneliness

We are social animals and need the support of others to prosper and survive. Independence may appeal to our political nature but it will not put food on the table. We must rely on others.

For example, you walk into the grocery store to buy some boneless skinless chicken breasts. More than likely, there are hundreds of people responsible for getting those chicken breasts to the market.

Fossil fuels go into the power plant to forge the steel that makes the farm equipment, that produces the feed, that is distributed by trucks to get to the chicken farmer who has help in raising the chickens that get shipped to the processing plant that processes the chicken which is then shipped to the warehouses of the grocery stores who eventually stock the items and have a check out and baggage clerk to deliver the boneless skinless chicken breasts. Meanwhile, the whole thing is underwritten by bank loans and protected by insurance.

Similarly, we rely on police, fire and medical people to protect us. We are part of a large interconnected social web. Yet with all of these people and all of these interactions we at times feel alone. We understand all human contact is not the same.

Psychologists observed people see themselves in three separate spheres:

1. Personal self
2. Social self
3. Collective self.

To use an academic example, at the personal level you as an individual may strive to get straight A's and hold a friendly competition with your siblings. You as the social self at the family level may take pride in your sibling getting a Rhodes scholarship. At collective level you root for your alma mater.

How you approach and react to people in your surroundings depend on what perspective you hold at the time. Psychologists studying loneliness found their data fit into similar spheres. They created three categories of social connection:

1. Intimate,
2. Relational
3. Collective.

These are connected to three different levels of your personal needs. You need to be affirmed at the personal level, be connected to a group of family and friends at the relational level, and to be a part of something bigger than yourself at the collective level.

Fulfilling your needs at one level does not necessarily satisfy your needs at a different level. If you feel loneliness at a personal intimate level, you will not necessarily satisfy that need by getting together with a bunch of friends.

Researchers did find that if people were unhappy at one level they usually were unhappy at the other levels. Conversely, happiness at one level tended to spread to the other levels.

You will meet your first connectedness challenge when you quit work. Long time work friends will be seen less. You will have less in common with those who remain at work. Camaraderie and your connection to something significant and something larger than you will be severed.

In most cases this need will not be easily replaced. You will be able to spend more time with your spouse and friends who are also retired. But, the nature of the work camaraderie and connection to something larger will be lost.

The next connectedness challenge you may face could be the loss of your spouse or life partner or close family members. The pain from this loss will not be fully made up by being involved with your friends or the community at large. Losses at the different social connection levels can be disorienting if left unattended.

The loss of connectedness can lead to loneliness. Researchers draw a distinction between loneliness and depression. They see loneliness more like a physical or emotional need similar to hunger and thirst. In loneliness you yearn to fulfill this need and become active in its pursuit. While depression is more of being withdrawn and you experience a loss of drive.

The yearning associated with loneliness may be part of the reason you may unexplainably find yourself eating a half gallon of ice cream, drinking a bottle of vodka or smoking like a chimney. The feeling of loneliness is a warning signal to you that you should not isolate.

Researchers link long periods of loneliness with a loss of executive function. This is the part of the brain in charge of self control. Long periods of isolation deteriorate self control. This leads to the sorts of bad behavior associated with health problems, increased disability and early death.

It is important for you to understand the pang of loneliness is a call to action. Just as you take action with your diet and physical and mental activity you need to take action with your social life. You can't sit and wait for a knock on the door or the phone to ring.

Connecting with Others

Global surveys show the overwhelming majority of people rate love, intimacy and social affiliation above wealth, fame and physical health as the most important contributors to happiness. Yet other surveys show, at any given time, nearly 20% of the population feels isolated enough to cause them unhappiness.

Too many times retirement planning focuses on the financial at the expense of the personal and social. If all of your focus is on investing and spending money it is easy to lose the scent of what makes you happy.

You know being connected to others is important. But, how do 13 million older people become isolated and clinically depressed? Why do so many people end up alone? How do you avoid being one of them?

As a social animal your survival depends on how you balance selfishness with generosity. You have a responsibility to take care of yourself yet you can't do it alone. You need to interact with others and your environment.

You have an impact on your environment and it impacts you. For example, you and another person approach the local fishmonger. The fishmonger has fish fillets caught this morning but still has similar filets from three days ago. You smile, act polite and show kindness to the fishmonger. The other person is demanding, belittling and curt. Guess who gets the three-day old fish?

The best way to avoid loneliness and isolation is to develop an active social strategy. Although researchers recognize being active in the three social connection levels is no guarantee that you will never be lonely or isolated, but activity does lower your chances of becoming isolated.

You can begin to define your participation in the three levels by identifying things you can do with your spouse, family, friends and groups. These categories of people can help you target how you will meet your social needs. You may or may not create relationships within each category, but you should be aware of how you will meet your particular intimate, relational and collective needs.

This does not mean you need to change your personality or nature to meet each of the connection levels. One level may be more important to you than another. It is more a matter of pursuing those connections that create a stable social support network.

If you are shy and reserved you don't need to try out for the lead in the community musical. You may feel uncomfortable and unwilling to take part in large groups or organizations. Instead, you can get involved in faith-based groups or link up with other non-profit organizations. You can be part of book clubs or hobby groups that focus on a common interest and ease the pressure on interactive social skills.

If you are active and outgoing your activities could be leading a fundraiser for some critical community need, campaign for president of some organization or lead the charge for some important personal cause. These activities could supplement your intimate and relational activities with those close to you.

However you choose to define your social strategy you can begin to create your social framework based on what the psychologists have identified as social needs met though social networks.

	Intimate	Relational	Collective
Spouse	X	X	
Family	X	X	X
Friends	X	X	X
Groups	X	X	

Research shows married people tend to be less lonely than single people. In most cases a spouse or life partner meets the intimate connectedness needs. Your spouse may also be your best friend. You may have the same friends and participate in the same groups. Together, you can meet your social needs for each level.

Or you can do some things with your spouse and other things with your friends and groups without your spouse. You may have a separate set of friends who do specific things. You may be part of a group your spouse prefers to avoid. Either way, each social need level can be met.

If you are not married you may find meaning and self-affirmation elsewhere. It may be your work or it could be a close family member or friend who knows and understands you. Without a spouse or life partner to cheer you on makes it more important you take the initiative to stay connected.

One example of how multi-level social interaction works can be found in of those living to age 100. Each of the groups studied have extensive family and friendship social connections. In one Asian group, the women hold weekly gatherings. This serves a number of purposes. One is to socialize. Here everyone keeps up on the gossip and the goings on of the village.

Another is mutual support. The women are available to help each other. If one family has a problem, the group works to resolve it. This reduces worry and solidifies the connectivity among the women. There is comfort in knowing help is available even though you may not need it.

Another value is to maintain tradition. Younger women are brought in at a junior or lower level as helpers. Over time they replace the older women and the group carries on.

You may not live in a village or have this type of connection available. Though you can create mini-versions of it. You may take part in bike riding gatherings, bird watching soirees and so on. You can create or carry on your family traditions. It is a matter of you taking the initiative to get together with your family and friends to pursue common interests.

Whatever activities you choose should be done on a regular basis. This helps you to stay connected. A side benefit is the healthy challenges or healthy competition with people you care about. You may want to maintain good habits, stay upbeat and look good just to show them you can do it and not let them get the better of you.

The regular get-togethers give you something to look forward to. You can collect stories, anecdotes and gossip between gatherings for sharing. You also get a sense of usefulness when you help others.

There are social organizations for everything in the U.S. You may have belonged to one or more. The organizations can be professional, such as one for teachers, engineers, or general contractors or it could be community based or interest based.

Studies show it is more important to be connected to any organization than it is the specific organization you are connected to. For example, researchers found those attending religious services at least once a month reduced their rate of death by nearly one-third.

More frequent attendance showed even a greater reduction of the risk of death. Part of this could be explained by those attending religious services tend to have healthier lifestyles or it could be the uplifting aspects of focused social gatherings.

Longlifers understand the need to avoid isolation. They initiate and support social contact on a regular basis. This does not mean you need to maintain a frenetic and harried lifestyle. It is more like you need to find your rhythm and stay continuously engaged with things outside your self.

The best physical activity is one done on a regular basis. So to with social activities. It takes some effort to keep your social connections together and not let them drift apart. Building solid social support now will help you transition through the Stages of Retirement later.

SAMPLE LONGLIFER SOCIAL PROFILE

Categories	Short Term Plan	Longlifer/Ideal
Primary Theme		
Family	Annual holiday gathering	Build tradition
	Visit out-of-town kids	College funding
	Take grandkids on trip	90th birthday party
Secondary Theme		
Adventure	Take 2 trips	Explore Asia & Africa
	Backpack Rockies	Create travel website
	Learn to sail	85th birthday abroad
	Winter in warmth	
Spouse	China Trip	Travel
	Weekly hike	Stay active
	Movies & Theatre	Together time
	Weekly dinner date	
Family	Visit kids	Connectedness
	Grandkids adventure	Get to know grandkids
	Monthly dinner	Attend family celebrations
	Connect with siblings	
Friends	Golf 2x week	Maintain common interests
	Weekly lunch	
	Social dinners	
Groups	Join social club	Improve community
	Active in church	Help those in need
	Join travel club	

The Longlifer system brings in specific attention to the Personal and Others' guideposts to ensure you stay aware of the things and people that make you happy. These need to be part of your retirement priorities and reviewed periodically. The Retirement Storm is bound to knock things around and you need to keep your priorities in order.

Chapter 6

LIFESTYLE
STEP 3(A) INCOME NEEDS

The majority of new retirees' biggest fear is outliving their money. Upon closer look, the basis for this fear is rarely determined by deliberate calculation. Mostly, it's a sense or a feeling that gives this fear its form.

What can cause them to outlive their money? Either they did not save enough to begin with or they spend too much. A third possibility is they are unprepared to effectively manage changes to their savings and expenses over time.

Over 70% of new retirees' state they are unprepared for twenty to thirty years in retirement. Yet many aren't doing anything about it. Those who don't prepare will be swept away by the coming Retirement Storm.

To effectively prepare for change you need to grab the controls over your savings and expenses. With the controls in hand you can steer your way through the storm. First you need to take a close look at defining the cost of your new lifestyle.

The better you understand what drives your expenses, the better you can manage them. The key drivers of your expenses can be broken down into three categories:

1. Previous commitments
2. Outside forces
3. Current decisions

You have made decisions in the past that lock you into certain fixed expenses today. You may have a mortgage or you may be locked into an insurance contract or you may be stuck with an investment that would be costly to sell today. There may be car payments and other sorts of consumer debt and other things you are obliged to maintain.

These things are a part of the cost of your lifestyle. They need to be recognized as things you can't change quickly or change without substantial cost. When the storm hits, these fixed commitments can weigh you down, for example if you can no longer pay your mortgage or car payments. Or they can keep you afloat like a low interest mortgage in a rising inflationary environment.

Outside forces are the things that can change how you spend your money. These include increased taxes, rising health insurance premiums, inflation, and life events that effect you and your loved ones. By their nature, they have a degree of uncertainty either in happening or in magnitude. These are things you need to anticipate and decide if you need to add something or change something in your plan.

Change you think is likely to happen needs to be included in your short-term plan. You may not have a current expense today that you may have in your first year in retirement. There may be a child's wedding or grandchild's college education that is not in your current spending plan but needs to be included in your coming expense plan.

If you can anticipate a change forthcoming you can prepare for it. This requires you to look two to three years out to see if there are any additional expenses or a change in expenses that should be dealt with today. Anticipating changes gives you flexibility to alter your course during the storm.

Previous commitments deal with the past, outside forces deals with the future and current decisions deal with the present. You have the most control over the decisions you make in the present. These will be the go-to areas of expenses should you need to cut back and form your first layer of defense against the coming storm.

You have a choice over many day-to-day decisions. You can choose not to spend money, spend more or spend less. You can go out to a restaurant and buy a $30 meal or a $10 meal. You can take a trip or defer it. You can buy premium brands or private labels. But, before you make those decisions, you need to know how much you are spending now and how much flexibility you have in what you spend.

You do this by defining the overall cost of your lifestyle. The Personal and Others' activities make up the first two parts of your lifestyle. They form the direction you want to go and the things you want to do in retirement.

The third part of your overall lifestyle cost is your basic living expenses. Basic living expenses form the support level for doing the fun things in retirement. These expenses include your home, auto, insurance, taxes and general living expenses. You have some degree of flexibility on how much you spend, but these expenses are the month-to-month grind that must be met.

Basic Living Expenses

You may think that since you know you spend $5,000 per month you have a handle on your expenses. What will you do if your savings takes a hit and provides $500 less per month? Where will you cut back?

Knowing you spend $5,000 is better than not knowing how much you spend. But it does not provide you with the level of control you need to maneuver through the storm. That information alone doesn't let you know whether to let off the accelerator or hit the brakes on your LPOD.

You may think if you just cut out restaurant meals you will cut expenses enough to meet the shortfall. But, what if your current spending on those meals is $300 per month and you need to cut $500? What do you do next?

One critical lever of control to successfully survive the Retirement Strom is to understand how you spend money. To some this may imply a budget and its implications of restraint and therefore should be avoided. Others will realize this information is useful and is a mechanism for control.

The first step to garner control is to categorize your spending. This can be done in countless ways but a good starting point is to develop categories that mimic where your money goes. Major credit card companies and large banks organize your spending by general categories and you can see where your money has gone.

You can look to year-end statements for your checking account and credit cards to begin the process. If you take a lot of ATM withdrawals and are unsure where all of that money goes, you can track those expenditures with a journal for a month or so. You may find you spend $300 on double shot, fat-free, soy milk lattes. This is good information to have.

As a new retiree you do not want to carry any consumer debt into retirement. All debt is risky. It needs to be paid first and in a rising interest rate environment debt service may cannibalize your other spending. For many new retirees living debt free will take some adjustment.

Your home mortgage may be the sole exception to a debt free life. Previous generations' retirees mostly paid off their mortgage prior to retirement. There were mortgage certificate burning parties. They were able to do this since most loans were low interest and they didn't need to refinance and they lived in their home for the full thirty year term of the mortgage.

New retirees faced sky high interest rates in the 1970s and early 1980s when they first started entering the home market. As interest rates came off these highs countless opportunities to refinance and to move up the real estate price ladder kept this generation on the move. Each time the new retiree moved or refinanced, the terms of the loan were extended.

In the last few years, many have refinanced yet again. Although this tended to result in lower monthly mortgage payments, a loan that may have had fifteen years to pay off now has been extended back to thirty years. Most people will not be able to pay off their mortgage during their lifetime without moving.

If you carry a mortgage into retirement what options do you have? There is no right or wrong answer. Mostly, it depends on tradeoffs you are comfortable making. Nevertheless, there are five basic strategies for you to consider:

1. **Keep Existing Mortgage** – If you recently refinanced and have a lock on a long term low fixed interest rate, this strategy can make sense. In general, once retired, it is harder to borrow money since you no longer have a paying job. This access to capital allows you to keep your savings and liquidity in tack better preparing you for the Retirement Storm. It also is a sound strategy should inflation come roaring back.

2. **Refinance**- This option makes sense if your current interest rate is higher than the current market rate for fixed mortgage rates and you will continue to live in your home for at least three years. It can also make sense if you have a variable home equity loan or credit card or other consumer debt you wish to pay off. You can consolidate those risky variable debts into a fixed mortgage.

   A third reason to refinance would be if you have a variable interest rate. Variable rate consumer debt and variable rate mortgages shift interest rate risk to you. Once retired you generally have a fixed income and your mortgage should be fixed. If you have a variable debt its potential to increase can squeeze you and force unpleasant lifestyle tradeoffs. This is not the time to increase financial risk with a variable rate mortgage.

3. **Mortgage as a Wealth Builder** - The basic concept here is you can get access to your home equity. This may produce cash to meet your lifestyle needs and some additional cash that can earn more money on your investments than you would pay on your increased mortgage.

   There is a need for some portion of your savings to grow in value. Inflation is the scourge of the fixed income crowd. Some portion of your overall wealth needs to be invested for growth but you should avoid borrowing to accomplish this.

Straddling your mortgage with your investments only can be done effectively if you earn more than the interest rate on your mortgage. This requires you to take on more investment risk than fixed rate mortgages. This strategy always carries the possibility of losing money on your investments while having an extra bill to pay.

4. **Pay off Mortgage** – This strategy helps you sleep better at night and is the safest as you no longer carry debt. You lower the likelihood of being forced to sell your home because you can't make the monthly payments. You also have locked up your wealth in an asset that tends to hold its value over time. The best scenario is you have paid off your mortgage while you worked and are not going to pay it off with a large lump sum at retirement.

   If you choose to use your savings to pay off your mortgage at retirement, then you need to look at the impact of using up a portion of your savings to accomplish this. First, it will be quite expensive if you use your IRA or 401(k) money to pay the mortgage as these funds are subject to ordinary income taxes.

   Second, if you sell appreciated assets you may have capital gains taxes to pay. Each alternative requires more than one dollar of savings to pay off one dollar of debt. There is also an impact on your available cash since now you would have less cash. Less cash generates less income.

   You may have paid off your mortgage and can sleep better at night at the expense of being less prepared for emergencies if you draw down too much of your savings.

5. **Move Down** – With this strategy you sell your current house and buy a smaller house and reinvest the difference. The new home can be debt free or at least the new mortgage can be substantially reduced. This strategy potentially can increase your income, lower your expenses and reduce overall risk.

Though you have to be ready to move and the move down strategy is subject to costs and market risks. You may not be able to sell your home for what you think it is worth. There is purchase risk in buying the next place and if you are to finance the deal, there is interest rate risk.

Another uncertainty to this strategy is for you to adapt to your new living arrangements. Family disruptions can occur. New social networks may be harder to build and the new location may be more appealing in your fantasy than in reality.

New retirees have lived with debt most of their lives and are more comfortable with it than their parents. There is always risk in debt as can be seen with the 2008-09 housing meltdown and banking crises. But if you know the risks of debt and handle it responsibly you still can manage your way through the storm.

Your basic living expense supports your Personal and Others' activities and added together complete the cost of your new lifestyle. Once these are added together, you can see if your retirement is affordable and subsequently sustainable.

Your basic living expenses can be broken down into a variety of categories. The categories should reflect how you think about your monthly expenses and can be done in great detail or in summary form. For our example the following categories will be used:

- Home
- Health
- Consumer Debt
- General Living
- Income Taxes

Your home expense includes your mortgage if any, or rent. It also includes all other associated expenses like maintenance, insurance, upkeep, association dues and utilities. These expenses are isolated as a cost center to let you know how your costs could change if you decide to move. It also forms the critical center of your lifestyle.

Health is a separate category because this may become one of your greatest expenses during retirement and the one most likely to shift out of control. Here you would include health insurance and all out of pocket health expenses including dental, vision, prescription drugs and so on.

This category helps you identify the impact of Medicare cost shifts and since its costs will tend to increase faster than inflation, appropriate inflation factors can be applied specifically to this category to measure the impact on your overall cost of living.

Consumer debt is separated because debt is a legal obligation. If you have any debt, such as car payments, home equity or other outstanding obligations these would still need to be paid should you have to cut back on your overall expenses due to some unforeseen event. Consequently, consumer debt reduces your flexibility in managing your expenses.

General living covers most of the rest of your spending. It excludes what you spend on your Personal and Others' activities as these are accounted for separately. It includes things like food, gas, car insurance, personal grooming, every day spending money and similar expenses. This category offers the most flexibility in responding to changing financial conditions as these expenses can be readily reduced or eliminated.

Income taxes take on a new role in retirement. You most likely will need to pay estimated quarterly income tax payments to both the Federal government and the State government if your state has an income tax. Failure to pay the proper amount results in penalties and interest expenses.

In estimating your income tax you need to be clear on the difference between your marginal tax rate and your average tax rate. Your marginal rate is the highest tax rate you pay but it is just applied to the amount above a certain level.

For example, let's say the tax rate for earnings above $75,000 is 28%; you would pay 28% only on your earnings above $75,000, not on the amount up to $75,000. If you use this higher rate on all of your earning you will vastly overstate the taxes you will pay and subsequently overstate the amount of money you need to retire.

Instead, for planning purposes, you should use your average tax rate. This can be quickly calculated by looking on your tax return for the total tax due. Then divide this amount by your adjusted gross income. This is not a substitute for figuring out your quarterly estimated payments, but it can be used for planning purposes.

Your total lifestyle expense lets you know what you need to spend, it does not tell you what you need to earn. These expenses are considered after tax expenses. You need to add taxes on top of these expenses to get your total amount of money you need to maintain your lifestyle.

For example, if you want to spend $4,000 per month after taxes and you have an average tax rate of 20% you will need to earn or withdraw $5,000 a month to net the $4,000 you plan to spend. Your mind needs to adjust to this higher monthly expense amount.

Now, all of the lifestyle components can be brought together to show you an example of what the cost of retirement would look like.

ESTIMATED LIFESTYLE COST

		Monthly	Annually
Personal			
	Family Travel	$	$ 1,000
	Adventure Travel	5,000	
	Golf, Tennis, Sailing	200	2,400
	Learning	<u>50</u>	<u>600</u>
	Total Personal	$ 250	$ 9,000
Social			
	Activities with Spouse	$ 200	$ 2,400
	Activities with Friends	150	1,800
	Social Club dues	<u>250</u>	<u>3,000</u>
	Total Social	$ 600	$ 7,200
Basic			
	Home	$2,000	$24,000
	Health	500	6,000
	Consumer debt	200	2,400
	General Living	<u>1,000</u>	<u>12,000</u>
	Basic	$3,700	$44,400
Total before taxes		$4,550	$60,600
Taxes – 15% average		$ 802	$10,700
Total		$5,352	$71,300
Annualized per month			$ 5,941

Most people think of their expenses on a monthly basis. This makes some sense in that most bills are paid monthly. Yet thinking of expenses on a monthly basis tends to imply your expenses, and your monthly budget, are fixed. They are not. Many of your monthly expenses vary from month to month. It is in this variability where risk and control lies.

If you are locked into a monthly number you limit your flexibility in managing your expenses by the illusion of rigidity. To manage your way through the storm you need flexibility and maneuverability. If you need to cut $500 per month from your budget, how would you do it? Or how do you know if you can afford that $5,000 trip to the Seychelles? To begin to answer these questions you need to take a new look at how you spend money.

Basis for Control

The better you can define something and the better you can understand its behavior, the better chance you have for controlling it. This works for how you spend money. The better you understand what drives your expenses the more control you have and the more secure you will feel in retirement.

To get a better sense of control you need to look at your expenses differently. Instead of a rigid monthly perspective where a necessary reduction in spending causes uncertainty and apprehensiveness, your new perspective sees alternatives and choices that can make adjustments manageable.

You can view your expenses as a series of concentric circles, or rings in a cut tree. The inner most circle covers your critical expenses, basic food, shelter and security. Each outlying ring adds a layer of protection and additional enrichment of your lifestyle.

With tree rings, the wider the space between rings indicates a better, healthier year for the tree, while narrow rings indicate tougher times. Similarly, in bountiful times, where your investments perform better than expected or you experience a drop in other expenses, you can expand your lifestyle to pursue specific retirement dreams. In tougher times, you can contract and weather out storms.

The coming storm is bound to leave some damages in its wake. You most likely will need to make changes in how you spend money. Some changes may be temporary while others may be permanent. Your decisions will be more effective when you make them within a proper perspective and knowledge of your options. You can do this by applying CPR to your expenses that is Choices, Priorities and Ranges.

Choices

At any time, your current position is less about how outside events affected you but more about your choices in response to those outside events. You live by the choices you have made. In retirement you choose to spend money or not spend money. You can spend less money or more money. Whatever choices you make in the moment will reverberate throughout your retirement.

One critical way of thinking about how you spend money in retirement is to think of expenses in a before-tax cost. For example, if you decide to buy a new car for $20,000, the true cost of the car is far above that amount. You need to remember that you will need to pay income taxes on the money you withdraw to pay for the car.

Now you may need to take out $25,000 from your savings to net the $20,000 you will pay for the car. An additional but subtle cost is the lost income you forego from withdrawing the $25,000. If you are earning 4% on your savings, you lose an additional $1,000 per year in earnings for the remainder of your retirement. The more you buy the less money you have to generate income.

When you were working spending had a different connotation. You earned your money and taxes were withheld. You either saved or spent what was left. Spending in itself did not trigger new taxes. Now in retirement, prior to spending any large amount, you will have to consider the tax consequence. You may take the money from your IRA or bank savings or your brokerage account. Each withdrawal has a tax impact.

If you need to cut spending, you choose what, where and how much to cut. Each reduction of spending has its particular impact on the quality of your life. If you do not have a good understanding of your expenses a forced reduction in spending can lead to a brain freeze on what to cut resulting in cutting everything and the feeling you are under siege.

If you understand your spending habits you can surgically trim your spending while lessening the impact on your lifestyle and quality of life. With decisions made, you are not under siege and can go confidently about your daily life.

Priorities

Most people have a number in mind when they think of their monthly expenses. Unfortunately, this number tends to be static and rarely includes periodic expenses like property taxes, income taxes and insurance. That static number also leads them into thinking things are more stable than they actually are.

You may carry such a number as an approximation of what you spend to maintain your lifestyle. Your actual spending may vary widely from month to month making it difficult to know if extra spending is to be expected or if you are going off track and need to make corrections.

If you need to suddenly cut $500 a month from your budget where would you cut? It is hard to cut when you only think in terms of a monthly budget. It offers no flexibility or provides any guidance on how to go about this task in an intelligent manner. If you are like most people, you just reign in all spending hoping it will be enough.

The retirement storm will batter your expenses. Sometimes inflation will raise your cost of doing things. Other times higher taxes or a shifting of medical costs will take more money. Or your income could drop requiring you to make spending adjustments.

Your monthly expenses will not be static. They will change and you need the ability to monitor and manage that change. If you lack the ability to monitor and manage change your likely reaction to spending cuts or a reduction in income is to hunker down never knowing if you cut enough or knowing how long you need to live this reduced lifestyle. In the mean time you miss out on what you wanted to do in retirement.

Instead, if you know the details of your spending and have a rational approach to how you spend and conserve your resources, you can better weather the storm through artful pruning. If you know specifically how you would cut $500 a month you can make the reduction and confidently go about your retired life. You can expand and reach your goals instead of hunkering down and retreating.

You may have in mind several escape routes should your house catch on fire. If the fire occurs in the kitchen you go one way, if it starts upstairs you go another. You most likely know what you would grab, what is important to preserve. Similarly, in retirement you need a mental escape route. One where you protect what is most important and sacrifices that which is less so to ensure you carry on.

You can do this by setting priorities among your expenses. The concentric circles are your starting point. Remember the things you found to be important in meeting your Personal and Others' goals is still important if you are to preserve your health, defer disability and engage with others. These activities need to be in the inner circles and not casually discarded.

Knowing your core expenses are covered provides you with a general sense of security. Your outer layers of spending can contract and expand to reflect current realities. You can contract certain spending when times are tough and expand when times are plentiful. You can live an active vibrant retirement when you have the ability to monitor and manage your expenses in an intelligent manner.

Setting priorities help you do this. To keep things simple, you can categorize your spending into three priorities:

1) Critical
2) Desirable
3) Discretionary

Your critical expenses are those included in your inner circle and are those necessary to survival. These include some base level of food, shelter, clothing and medical expenses. It also includes some spending and activities necessary to maintain your physical, mental and social well being.

Desirable expenses are those that add quality to your life and you would prefer to continue to make these expenses. These include entertainment, hobbies, social activities and expanded levels of food, clothing and well being expenses.

Discretionary expenses are those that are nice but you could live without. These include recreational travel, sport shopping and various forms of luxury that add flavor to your retirement but in a pinch, you can do without.

Priorities help map out your expense escape routes. It reminds you what is important and what can be left behind. Knowing you have the ability to reduce expenses to various levels and remain secure when times are tough helps you confidently go about your daily life in normal or abundant times.

Ranges

Just because an expense is a top priority doesn't mean it is entirely sacrosanct. You choose what you spend on food whether it is truffles and caviar or hot dogs and chips or what you spend on clothing whether you shop at exclusive designer boutiques or the local thrift shop. There is a range of what you can spend. Knowing your range offers you flexibility and options when the storm hits.

Some expenses have wide ranges like food, clothing and entertainment. These offer you the most flexibility should you need to temporarily cut expenses. Other expenses have a narrow range like housing, insurance and taxes and to reduce these expenses requires major adjustments to your lifestyle and generally are left as the last resort.

To reduce housing, you need to move. To reduce insurance, you need to take on more risk. To reduce taxes, you need to take less taxable income. This leaves the bulk of your maneuvering to those expenses which have the widest range or to those expenses like travel that can be postponed.

The example above shows a monthly and yearly expense plan. Next you need to apply CPR to your plan.

EXPENSE PLAN

	Lean Times		Abundant Times
	Lower Range	Normal	Upper Range
Priority 1 – Critical			
Food	$ 400	$ 650	$ 1,000
Clothing	0	100	500
Personal Activities	100	250	400
Others' Activities	100	150	600
Housing	1,800	2,000	2,200
Health	450	500	500
Consumer Debt	250	250	500
Total Priority 1	$3,150	$3,900	$ 5,700

EXPENSE PLAN

	Lean Times		Abundant Times
	Lower Range	Normal	Upper Range
Priority 2 – Desirable			
General Living	$ 200	$ 400	600
Personal Activities	0	150	300
Others' Activities	0	100	400
Total Priority 2	$ 200	650	1,300
Priority 3 – Discretionary			
General Living	$ 0	$ 100	$ 500
Personal Activities	0	300	1,000
Others' Activities	0	100	500
Total Priority 3	$ 0	$ 500	$ 2,000
Total Range	$3,450	$5,050	$ 9,000

This is the sample monthly expense plan with your priorities and ranges set before income taxes. If you begin each year with your expense plan, set priorities and establish ranges you have a much better mindset going into the year. You know what you plan to do and know your options ahead of time should something go awry.

If you face an unexpected expense or if your savings suffer a temporary loss you can make intelligent adjustments as opposed to giving in to the emotional confusion of the moment. You also will know if you reduced your expenses enough so you can go about living your life as opposed to hunkering down and hoping for the best.

Control

You can't manage what you don't understand. You can't control what you can't manage. One crucial tool you have to exert control over your retirement is your expense plan. Some people have a hard time facing their expenses. They may not want to surface some obsession or forego the protection of denial on how much they are actually spending. Their reasons are best left to the psychologists.

To begin management and control over your retirement you must begin with your expense plan. Your expense plan should cover the next calendar year. You need to specify where you are spending money and how much you are spending. What you spend then needs to be linked to how you want to live out your retirement.

Management begins by knowing how flexible your plan is. If you don't adequately understand your expenses you can't reduce them in an intelligent manner. This tends to lead you into a financial seizure when the storm damages your lifestyle. You will find yourself unsure as to what expenses to cut or if your cuts are enough to offset the damage and yet remain secure throughout your retirement.

You can avoid this state of apprehensiveness through CPR. You have a high degree of control over your lifestyle costs with your Choice of whether or not you spend money. Your Priorities are linked to your retirement objectives and the Range of your expenses provides the flexibility to steer through the storm debris.

Your expense plan gives you target numbers on how you plan to spend money. With your plan set, you can compare what you actually spend during the year with what you planned to spend. This lets you know if specific spending is veering out of control or if things are going according to plan. Your expense plan is a powerful retirement tool providing critical information to make intelligent decisions.

But, if the storm hits you with something unexpected, you need to have prepared a contingency plan, your mental fire escape, ahead of time to intelligently direct your response. CPR helps you do this. It identifies potential spending cuts when you are in an objective state of mind, not in a state of crises and offers you options so you can remain in control

Your contingency plan should include pre-planned monthly spending cuts of 5%, 10% and 20% magnitude. This lets you start the year knowing you have a sustainable expense plan but should the unexpected hit you are better prepared knowing how you would reduce spending ahead of time. Avoiding such decisions in times of crises tends to lead to better decisions.

In step 1 you laid out your Personal desires and goals. Next, in step 2 you identified how you want to connect with Others'. You know you need to stay involved in activities that will keep you mentally and physically strong and socially connected. Keeping these things as priorities will help you intelligently reduce expenses should the storm batter your lifestyle.

Step 3a, Income, helps you quantify your overall cost of your preferred lifestyle. It identifies how much income you need. You now have an expense plan that can be tested against the income you can generate to see if it is sustainable. You have options and a sense of your flexibility to respond to the unexpected.

EXPENSE AND ACTIVITY PLAN

Planned Monthly Expense		**To Do Activity List**
Personal Activities	$ 750	**Personal**
Others' Activities	600	Daily walk
Home	2,000	Golf weekly
Health	500	Tennis twice weekly
Consumer Debt	200	Religious practice
General Living	1,000	Learn Mandarin
Total	$5,050	Backgammon
		Study astronomy
Income taxes @15%	$ 891	Creative activities
		Gardening
Total Monthly Expense	$5,941	Mediterranean Diet
Contingency Plan		**Others**
5% ($250)		Movie/Theatre
Food expense	$100	Weekly dinner date
Discretionary spending	150	Visit live away kids
		Grandkid adventure
10% ($500)		Family dinners
Above cuts plus		Lunch with friends
Golf & Tennis	$100	Religious activities
Restaurants	150	Sport activities
20% ($1,000)		
Above cuts plus		
Defer pleasure travel		

Your Expense and Activity Plan gives you a quick oversight of the year ahead. You have a general sense of what you will spend, a list of activities you wish to undertake and contingency plans should you encounter unexpected hits to your lifestyle.

In the above example, food and out-of-pocket expenses are the first line of defense when cutting lifestyle costs. This is where it helps for you to know where your money goes. The better expense detail you have the more surgically you can cut expenses that have the least impact on the overall quality of your life. The better detail lets you shed the less important items first.

Knowing how you want to live and how you spend money gives you the control over the steering, gas pedal and brakes of your LPOD. In good times you can accelerate and steer towards the things you may have put off while in tougher times you can brake and slow your momentum to steer away from trouble.

When you keep in mind the activities you hold important, those that help you defer disability and remain intellectually and physically strong and socially connected, helps you make more intelligent decisions on where to reduce spending.

Linking your activities with your expenses offers you additional control as you now know how to steer your LPOD through the storm debris. The Expense and Activity Plan gets imbedded into the instrument panel of your LPOD helping you to manage your retirement. When you understand this part of your retirement you are better prepared for the unexpected that will likely occur through the Stages of Retirement.

Chapter 7

INCOME
STEP 3 (B) INCOME SOURCES

You can maneuver more successfully throughout your retirement when you have reliable and sustainable sources of income. It's easy to get confused whether your lifestyle should be constrained by your income of if you should try to generate more income to meet your new lifestyle.

While you worked your income ultimately constrained your lifestyle. There may have been times where you spent more than you earned. Yet there had to have been more times where you spent less than you earned to have saved anything for retirement.

Once you retire you need to think differently about how you earn and spend money. You no longer have a steady predictable paycheck about which your spending can oscillate. This leaves potential shortfalls to be covered by depleting your savings.

Instead of having future paychecks to cover today's shortfalls you now must rely on your savings. When you take more from your savings than it has earned you not only deplete principal you also forego future income from your savings leaving you more vulnerable as you age.

Once you retire, your income is redefined away from a single source paycheck to multiple sources of Social Security, employer pensions and savings. Social Security and pensions may be reliable in the short term, but they alone won't sustain your lifestyle over time. Income from your savings can be sustainable over time if you take out less than you earn, but the income stream will vary and be less reliable.

Old retirees were able to cover 69% of their lifestyle costs through Social Security and employer pensions. New retirees can expect those sources to cover roughly 33% of their lifestyle. The rest of your lifestyle costs need to be covered by your personal savings. Social Security and pensions are designed to make payments for the rest of your life but you can outlive your personal savings.

Research shows a link between reliable, predictable income and happiness. When retirees' predictable income is at least 25% of their lifestyle expense they report a boost in retirement satisfaction of 70%.

Those who had a greater portion of their monthly expense covered by guaranteed income exhibited fewer depression symptoms. At any income level, those who had a greater portion of guaranteed income perceived themselves to have more money than those with less guaranteed income even when their total wealth was the same.

This makes sense in a couple of ways but misses a larger point. A larger stream of guaranteed income lowers the risk of meeting your expenses. It also provides you a sense of comfort that some minimal amount of money will come in regardless of circumstances. A fixed dollar amount can be deceiving if inflation and taxes erode it over time.

In retirement your biggest challenge may be to generate income. Much of what is in the popular press emphasizes this point. It tends to direct your focus towards investment strategies and products. But, while the media has you focused on your investments and income, unattended expenses and personal needs can spring a leak in your net worth.

Your thinking in retirement needs to evolve from simply managing your savings and investments to managing the balance between your income sources and your lifestyle expenses. It's the connection and the equilibrium between the two that you need to manage over time if you are to weather the storm. Over emphasis on one at the expense of the other tilts you off balance and increases the chances of you being blind sided by what otherwise would be a manageable event.

{Uncertainty} Income Sources ←---------→ Income Needs {Uncertainty}

Your income sources and income needs are shadowed by different degrees of uncertainty. Your income needs will change over time. Inflation, life expectancy, health, disability, capital and repair expenses among other things can change your spending patterns. If your income needs rise unexpectedly you must decide whether to cut expenses elsewhere or take more money from your savings.

Your income sources also are affected by uncertainty. Taxes, cuts in Social Security and employer pension benefits, inflation, investment market volatility, interest rates, and political and economic changes can reduce your spending income. These outside uncertainties can cause once reliable income to become less so.

You may start your retirement in balance, but your challenge will be to stay in balance. Unexpected rises in your income needs or reductions in your sources of income will require you to make adjustments. Linking your sources and needs allows your retirement plan to signal you when something needs attention.

If something unexpected happens you may need to decide to reduce expenses or invade principal. You'll need to decide if the change is temporary, long term or permanent. The results of your decisions flow through your income sources and income needs continually shifting the balance between them.

When your focus is on this balance, you can more readily respond in a timely and effective manner. You can make intelligent changes and restore balance. Uncertainties are bound to happen during your retirement. Keeping your income sources and needs in balance keeps you buoyant through the storm.

The Expense and Activity Plan helps you manage your income needs, now its time to look at how to manage your income sources.

Social Security

You'll need to make two critical and likely irreversible decisions when you qualify for Social Security. If you are married, you'll need to decide if your spouse will be added to your monthly income benefit and if you're married or single, you'll need to decide when to start your benefits.

When considering whether to add your spouse to your income stream you need to look at the total benefits to the household and the reduction in the risk of either of you outliving your assets. In general, you should include your spouse on your Social Security income stream.

If you add your spouse you get a lower monthly benefit but it should last for a longer period of time. This reduces the chance of your spouse outliving your household assets. Statistically, you end up with the same total household benefit since two people have a greater chance of at least one of them living to life expectancy.

If you choose not to add your spouse you will have a higher monthly benefit. But if you die before life expectancy you end up with less household benefits and you shift the investment risk of producing income to your surviving spouse.

Social Security is one source of income that guarantees monthly payments for both of your lives. You can outlive your other assets. The reassurance of both of you receiving some minimum amount of lifetime income provides a safety net and a base level to your financial security. Adding your spouse is a cost-effective way to reduce the risk of lost income.

There are some cases where you may not want to include your spouse on your benefit stream. One case would be if your spouse is severely ill and is unlikely to out live you. Another would be if your spouse is significantly older. A third would be if your spouse has sufficient assets and the additional income is not needed.

Deciding when to begin your benefits is a bit more complicated. At first, this would seem to be an easy decision. The sooner you start receiving your benefits the better. As with most things governmental, it's not that simple.

You'll need to make a personal decision on two critical but uncertain factors. The first is how long you will live. The second is whether your benefits will be cut before or during your retirement.

Your starting point balances around the fulcrum of what is considered full retirement. If you were born between 1943 and 1954 full retirement is age 66. The full retirement age increases steadily to age 67 for those born between 1954 and 1959. Currently, it's age 67 for those born after 1960.

If you start your benefits early, they will be reduced by an average 6 ¼% per year where the benefits are 25% lower at age 62. To the contrary, benefits are increased at 8% a year for starting points from age 67 to age 70.

Sample Monthly Benefits Array

Age 62	Age 66	Age 70
$750	$1,000	$1,320

Your choices range from taking a smaller monthly amount for a longer period of time or a higher amount for a shorter period of time. The best decision is based on how long you think you will live. The benefits are about equal if you live to life expectancy. If you think you will live longer, delaying to get the higher monthly amount could result in more money.

The benefits are calculated around life expectancy. If you make it to age 65 your average remaining life expectancy is 18 years or age 83. Once you make it to 65 you have a 25% chance of living to age 90 and a 10% chance of living to age 95.

If you start your benefits at age 62 you would have received $36,000 ($750 mo*48mo) before you would have received anything if otherwise you waited to age 66 to begin taking your benefits. If you start your benefits at age 66 you get an additional $250 a month.

In simple terms it would take you 144 months ($36,000/$250) or twelve years to breakeven. Once you past age 78 you would end up with more dollars from Social Security when you start your benefits at age 66...

If you are confident you'll live beyond age 78, you generally will get more money by starting your benefits later even if you make the adjustment for the timing of the payments. But again it is not that simple. You need to factor in what you would do with the $36,000 you would have received if you started the benefits earlier.

If you use that money to pay your monthly bills, you take less money from your savings leaving you with a higher savings balance. If you don't need the money to pay your bills, you can save the money thus increasing your savings balance. What's the value of those early payments?

If you earn 3% after tax, the $9,000 a year you receive for the first four years would total roughly $37,600 extra in your savings. Again at 3% your increased savings balance would generate an additional $94 a month from age 66 and beyond if you chose to start your benefits at age 62. Your total potential income would be $844 ($750 + $94) versus the $1,000 you would get waiting to start your benefits at age 66.

It's not just earning back the $36,000 in extra money but the lifetime income stream off the $36,000. This changes your breakeven from 12 years to over 19 years and you would have to live past age 85 to breakeven. If you think you can earn more money on the additional savings the breakeven is longer.

One key skill you'll need to enhance during retirement is managing risk. If you wait to take your benefits you will get more money over the long term but you take on the risk of not living long enough to get the benefits. You also take on the risk of Social Security benefits being cut in the future thus changing your calculations. Finally, you take the risk you can earn the monthly income you are deferring elsewhere.

Gale force winds from the coming storm are shaking the foundation of Social Security. Its foundation was never particularly strong to begin with. Franklin Roosevelt who signed the act into law expressed concerns of the long-term ability to keep it financed.

When the baby boomers hit the job market in the 1960's and 1970's the cleverness of using payroll taxes to fully fund Social Security became evident to politicians. The payroll taxes were mixed with general revenues allowing politicians to pander to voters by steadily expanding coverage to disability, survivorship, and cost-of-living increases being the most prominent

Congress quickly redirected the payroll taxes from funding Social Security to paying for current budget deficits. This quickly tilted the system towards default in the early 1980s. In 1983 comprehensive reform of Social Security was supposed to fix the system.

The so-called permanent fix turned out to be temporary. It consisted of a combination of increased payroll taxes and decreased benefits, mostly affected by increasing the age of full retirement. To prevent Congress from diverting payroll taxes to fund the current budget a Social Security Trust fund was established to ensure the contributions would be there for your retirement.

It didn't take long for Congress to figure out how to get at the cash. It simply took the cash from the trust fund in exchange for Treasury notes and bonds. This allowed Congress to borrow money easily without going to the global financial markets. The borrowings from the trust fund are off-the-books, that is, Congress doesn't need to show them as an ongoing debt of the government.

All very clever until the deception and faults buried in the system gets exposed. The deception is Congress took the cash and there is no money in the trust fund. To get money to pay future retirees, Congress will have to go to the financial markets to borrow more money. This will be on top of the trillions recently borrowed to bail out the banks, car companies, insurance companies and stimulus for special interests.

The fault in the system is the way it's funded. It counts on shifting money from current workers to retirees. As long as there are a lot more current workers than retirees the game can go on. The taking of money from one group of people and giving it to another with the hope this can be done indefinitely has been compared by some to a Ponzi scheme.

This may be a little harsh but not completely off course. You probably read the stories of Bernie Madoff. He ran the largest discovered Ponzi scheme ever defrauding victims of billions of dollars. He would take money from new investors to meet redemptions of old investors. As long as new money came in faster than money going out no one was wiser. This let him keep the difference while investing little or nothing. The scheme was exposed when the new money dried up and current investors began withdrawing more money.

The current system is like a diamond standing on end. The longest section across the diamond represents the baby boomer generation. The much bigger section can support the top of the diamond. But, when the boomer generation retirees, they in turn will need to be supported by a much smaller section.

It won't take long for the system to collapse under its own weight. Cracks in the foundation are showing up sooner than expected. The Great Recession dumped a lot of people in their early sixties onto the unemployment line. With prospects for getting a job slim, many of these people opted for early retirement forcing Social Security into deficits.

The 2010 Trustees' report put a happy face on things by using overly generous assumptions on economic growth and employment to claim the fund can survive until 2037. Its survival to 2037 is based on cash flow accounting, that is, more money coming in from workers than going out to retirees not on what is actually owed retirees.

The Trustees' report loses some of its comfort should unemployment stay high and economic growth slow. Even with their generous assumptions, the fund is likely to run dry sometime during your retirement unless changes are made.

What are the likely changes and how will they affect you? The entire system needs to be completely redesigned. The political will is probably not there. This leaves four potential options:

1. Raise payroll taxes
2. Raise income and other general taxes
3. Inflate the economy
4. Cut benefits

Each has severe drawbacks. Raising payroll taxes would likely increase unemployment and further undermine the financial stability of the system. It would also pit parents against children to see who will pay the retirement tab. Raising income taxes will have its own resistance groups and would likely slow economic growth thus lowering employment.

Inflating the economy would allow the government to meet its future dollar obligations with dollars that are worth less. From 2008 to 2011 the Federal Reserve has been printing money and flooding the financial system with cash. History shows this almost always leads to an increase in inflation 18 to 24 months later. Inflation has its own political consequences one being Social Security is indexed to inflation and its cost would increase.

Reducing benefits, especially near retirement would create a large and vocal opposition of nearly the entire boomer generation. Congress can cut benefits for younger workers by raising the retirement age; it can reduce or eliminate cost-of-living increases, raise the amount of Social Security subject to income taxes and cut actual monthly benefits.

In all likelihood you'll see some combination of the four. Before any major change, effective organizations prepare those affected through a variety of warning signs. Private employers tend to talk about how bad business is that profits are down and the competition is getting tougher months before they begin layoffs and firings.

The government is currently doing this with Social Security. There is a debt commission tasked with reviewing all options available including cutting entitlements, raising taxes and cutting other government spending. The most ominous sign is discussing Social Security as an entitlement.

If perception is changed to view Social Security as an entitlement it opens the door to cut benefits for those who are financially better off. Social Security could then be viewed as a form of welfare and that it should only be available for those in financial need.

But you have been having money taken from your paychecks for the last thirty to forty years and should be under the impression you were saving for retirement. You and your employer likely contributed somewhere between $200,000 and $600,000 over that time. This should be viewed as your savings and not that you are some welfare case unjustly receiving a handout.

The writing is on the wall. Some form of change will happen over the next several years. The coming storm will affect your benefits for the entire period of your retirement. Should you be concerned? How vulnerable are you to cuts in benefits?

The more dependent you are on receiving the monthly benefits the more vulnerable you are to cuts. If Social Security covers a large portion of your monthly living expenses and if you don't have adequate savings, you are more vulnerable than if the benefits are considered a small portion of your income and wealth.

Your vulnerability can be measured by the Social Security Vulnerability Index (SSVI). It measures the importance of your benefits to your monthly income and your savings. Both the income and saving sides need to be considered. If benefits are cut you would need to take more money from your savings to maintain your standard of living. A further reduction in your savings means your money won't last as long as it otherwise would.

You can calculate your SSVI as follows:

You can calculate your SSVI as follows:

$$\left\{1+ \frac{\text{Monthly Benefit}}{\text{Monthly Expense}} \quad X \quad (1+ \frac{\text{Annual Benefit})^2}{\text{Total Savings}} -1\right\}$$

For example if your benefit is $1,000 a month and your monthly expenses are $3,000 a month and your total savings is $240,000 your SSVI is:

$$\left\{1+ \frac{1,000}{3,000} \quad X \quad (1+ \frac{12,000)^2}{240,000} -1\right\}$$

$$\{1.33 \, X \, (1.05)^2 -1\} = .47$$

The scale to put this number into perspective is:

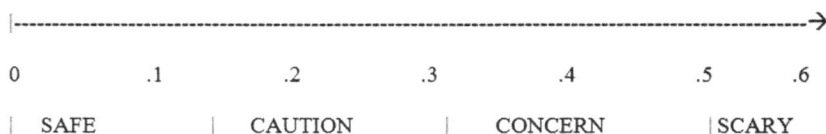

|---→

| 0 | .1 | .2 | .3 | .4 | .5 | .6 |

| SAFE | | CAUTION | | CONCERN | |SCARY |

SSVI measures your vulnerability to reductions in your benefits, not its actual impact. You can be vulnerable to change but the change itself needn't be catastrophic. The more vulnerable you are only means that you likely will need to make a change to your retirement plan should your benefits be cut.

For example, if your benefits are cut by $100 per month you may readily adjust your other expenses to cover the shortfall. Or you might be able to take the amount from your savings with little or no impact. In the case you need to make an adjustment to your plan but the cut can be accommodated without a drastic change to your lifestyle and financial security.

If the $100 benefit cut means you now need to choose between food and medicine your vulnerability could be life threatening. The SSVI is one measurement gauge on the dashboard of your LPOD. An actual cut will reverberate throughout your plan and its overall effect will be captured by the evaluation process.

If you have yet to begin collecting your Social Security, the choice of starting your benefits early or waiting is not a clear-cut decision. One choice is not necessarily better than the other. You need to decide which option better serves your needs.

If you delay payments you will get more money if you live beyond age 83. But, you take the risk of not living long enough to start benefits and the risk that you won't survive past the breakeven period.

If you start benefits earlier you may end up with less money overall, but you shed the risk of life expectancy and you get money now. There is no certain best decision, just one that is better or less bad.

Consider taking your benefits early if:
- You need the money
- Your SSIV is high
- Your savings are low
- You don't expect to live to life expectancy
- You have the skills and discipline to invest unneeded benefit money
- You expect large cuts to benefits

Consider delaying your benefits if:
- You are still working in your mid and late 60's
- You have substantial savings
- Your benefit covers a small part of your overall monthly expense
- You expect to live beyond age 83
- You want to leave a higher benefit to your surviving spouse.

Social Security provides income you can't outlive. You don't have investment risk, though there is some political risk. Social Security can be a cornerstone to your retirement income foundation, a building block. But, it was never designed to be your sole source of income.

Private Employer Pension Plans

Some new retirees will qualify for an employer monthly retirement benefit, most will not. Originally, employer pensions were designed to complement Social Security offering workers additional lifetime income. This would help workers maintain a modest standard of living in retirement should something unfortunate happen to them or their savings.

Two major events occurred in the 1980's that changed the perception of the value of pension plans. First was the realization that companies now faced severe global competition. Second, was the accounting requirement that the value of the future promises to workers for both pensions and retiree health costs now be included on the company's balance sheet as a long-term liability.

Initial pension plans were designed to attract and retain employees. It was thought employees' skills increased over time and became more valuable to the company. Also, if valued employees were offered a pay raise by another company, they would have to consider losing their pensions and make the decision to leave harder.

Global competition made this rigid personnel policy ineffective. Companies now needed to the ability to make staffing changes quickly to remain competitive. Downsizing became the euphemism for firings, layoffs and early retirement buyouts.

The value of the pension benefit was mostly determined by how long the employee worked at the company and the salary earned in the last five or so years of employment. This meant the longer employees worked at the company the more the retirement benefits cost the company. On the other side, workers who had to change jobs never were able to build up a meaningful benefit.

Having to recognize the costs of retiree promises on its balance sheets worsened the company's overall financial position. This had a tendency to erode credit ratings, raise interest costs and overall make raising capital for the company more costly. The liability needed to be managed.

Companies realized they were liable for poor investment performance of the pension assets and the newly recognized increases in life expectancy. If investments were poor, the company had to take more of its profits and add them to the retirement plan. This was an element the company could not control and it no longer wanted the risk.

These two critical events shaped the shift from the employer providing a monthly lifetime benefit to offering workers 401(k) plans and money purchase plans. These plans shifted investment risk to workers and made employer matching contributions predictable and discretionary for the employer. The employer now had greater control over this growing cost.

Although you may be entitled to an employer monthly benefit retirement plan, it is not without risks. You face the same decision process on whether to have your spouse on the benefit stream and the timing of starting your benefits.

As with Social Security, you face a potential reduction in future benefits. A recent review of companies making up the S&P 1500 shows their pensions plans under funded by over $400 billion dollars. These plans now cover only 75 cents on each dollar of benefits or 75% of its obligations.

Pension consultants consider plans funded less than 80% as endangered. Additionally, nearly half of all unions are similarly under funded to be considered endangered. The only way these funds can be rehabilitated is with some combination of substantial increases in the financial markets and cash contributions.

Neither is likely in the near term as the country struggles with the recession and financial mess. This has led some companies to terminate or freeze their plans. If your plan is terminated or frozen you no longer will see your benefits increase. They will be locked in on the date or termination or freeze. If you were counting on getting a higher benefit from your employer, you now will have to make up the difference yourself.

Other companies, having paid premiums to cover default, have opted to file bankruptcy and dump their retirement plans on the government. The Pension Benefit Guarantee Corporation (PBGC) is the entity responsible for managing those plans. They are responsible for collecting premiums and managing the risk of companies defaulting on their pension obligations.

Unfortunately, the PBGC recently announced a tripling of its deficit from $11 billion to $33 billion dollars. It's woefully unprepared to take over any more pension plans. Yet, bankruptcy and shedding pension obligations may be the only choice for desperately struggling companies. Will this create another bailout?

If PBGC does take over your plan you still may not get dollar-for-dollar coverage. It has formulas to determine how much it will pay out. Generally, it caps annual benefits at around $42,000 a year. If your benefit is larger you lose the difference. Also, there is the possibility it will lower the cap to help it resolve its deficits.

Companies want to avoid the liability and risk of guaranteeing lifetime income to its retired employees. They will help you to save for retirement, but ensuring an income stream becomes your responsibility.

Even if your company will provide you with a lifetime income stream you need to consider whether the company can meet its obligations over the 20 to 30 years you will be in retirement. Once you choose your retirement option you are locked in.

Some companies allow for a lump sum distribution of your retirement benefits. If you chose this option you avoid the implications of your employer going out of business but you take on the investment risk.

With a lump sum distribution, your employer gives you one large check for the entire value of your retirement benefit. You can rollover this amount into an IRA and continue to defer income taxes. You then would make your investment decisions.

One alternative to taking on investment risk would be to turn over your lump sum to an insurance company in return for an annuity to provide a lifetime income stream. This would make sense if you want a guaranteed income stream and if you feel your employer is financially weaker than the insurance company.

Similar to taking a lump sum distribution is to rollover your 401(k) into an IRA account. Some employers allow you to leave your account with them when you leave or retire. Leaving it lets you hold familiar investments at possibly a lower cost then moving your account to a brokerage firm.

If you rollover your account to a brokerage firm you need to complete a direct transfer from your employer to the brokerage firm. The brokerage firm will help you with the paperwork. If you take the withdrawal personally you are subject to withholding taxes. This is money that you can't get back until you file your following years' tax return. Avoid this unless you are desperate for cash.

The 401(k) rollover allows you to continue to defer taxes and it opens up the universe of investments. You'll have many more investment choices at a brokerage firm than with your employer. If you don't want the investment risk, like the lump sum choices above, you can convert your 401(k) to an annuity with an insurance company.

Government Pension Plans

Government operational practices tend to lag the private sector. Lacking the profit motive and having easy access to taxpayers' dollars tend to take the urgency out of making operation improvements. Where the private sector needs to be competitive, the public sector tends to be political.

Yet, at some point, even the government gets constrained by financial realities. Its taken about 30 years for the government to figure out the pension promises it makes are not sustainable.

Federal, state and local governments let employees retire earlier and with a higher level of benefit than most private sector employers. How has government been able to keep these plans going? They simply under funded them. Now, the storm is sweeping through.

For example, Illinois has $54.4 billion in unfunded pension liabilities. The same 80% rule applies to determine when a fund is endangered. Illinois funding level is 54%. It's not alone. A recent study showed state pension funds lost $865 billion nationwide due to the financial collapse. How will this shortfall be made up?

To make matters worse, the accounting rule requiring private employers to show the liability of their pension promises on their balance sheet will soon be required of public entities. In the past, the public sector simply didn't put enough money into the plans to keep them going. These shortfalls have been accumulating for decades.

But, the financial collapse and the accounting change brings the under funded status of pensions to the forefront. The shortfalls become real when the massive number of new retirees begin collecting their benefits. One study showed a trillion-dollar gap between the pension and health care benefits promised and the money set aside to pay for them.

Various agencies have begun to discuss changes to their pension rules. Increasing the age of full retirement, lower benefits to future employees and something similar to a 401(k) in lieu of monthly benefit plans are being discussed.

A number of states are going to court to reduce benefits to current employees and retirees. What was once thought of as a guarantee may no longer be. Some courts have ruled benefits can be reduced for current retirees only when the government employer is on the brink of insolvency. This is currently happening to a number of small cities and counties throughout the country.

Minnesota is trying to take the ability to reduce benefits one step further. Its claiming retirees have no legal right to a specific formula of benefits. The benefits should be subject to reasonable legislative action to preserve the integrity of the plan for all participants. If this holds, benefit formulas can be redesigned to provide lower benefits to everyone.

If you are a government employee or retiree, there now is some doubt to the reliability of getting your promised monthly lifetime benefit. Like potential cuts to Social Security, you'll need to asses your vulnerability to potential benefit cuts.

This is bound to open a political battle between taxpayers and government retirees as the new accounting rules demand more funding for pensions. Governments would have to cut their budgets elsewhere, creating various opposition, and/or raise taxes. One county in California needs an additional $100 million a year just to pay the pensions it owes.

It will be hard to raise taxes on secretaries, mechanics and other middle income tax payers to fund pensions of retirees that may be more than the middle class makes working. The retirement storm is churning uncertainty everywhere.

Income Taxes

Where there's income there's taxes. When you worked you probably had little flexibility in determining your taxable income. You got your paycheck and some interest income from savings accounts and that less 401(k) contribution set your taxable income. You tallied up your deductions and ended up with a tax bill.

If you were self employed or owned your own business you had more flexibility in determining your income and deductions. If your business was a corporation you had more than one tax pocket to play with and probably spent some time attempting to legally lower your taxes.

In retirement you'll also have more than one tax pocket to play with. Income taxes may very well be one of your largest budget items and it will need attention and management. The more you pay in taxes the less you have for your lifestyle and savings.

No matter how well you build your retirement foundation or how well you seal your LPOD, the coming storm by continually battering your structure will erode it severely over time. Though income taxes are irritatingly complex, your quality of life will be better if you can effectively manage your tax obligations.

If you are like most retirees, you have an IRA or 401(k), some personal savings, Social Security and possibly a pension. Each of these can be viewed as a tax pocket. Each pocket has difference tax consequences. Taking money out of one pocket can cost more than taking it out of another pocket. You can view the tax pockets as having spigots. You can turn the flow on and off although your Social Security and pensions can only be turned on.

TAX POCKETS

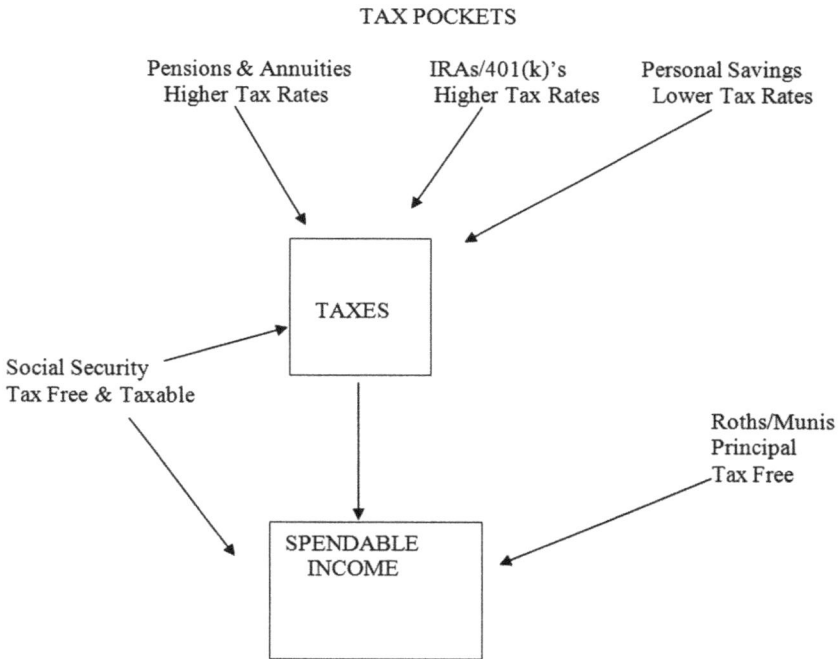

Social Security is currently tax free up to certain income levels. The rules use the broadest definition of income. It grabs all global income including pensions and adds tax exempt interest, Roth withdrawals and other forms of income generally not considered taxable. When all of these are added together, it gets compared to thresholds to determine if you are required to pay tax on your benefits.

If you are single and all of your other earnings are less than $25,000, your Social Security benefits are not taxable. However, if you earn between $25-34,000 half of your benefits are taxed and if you earn over $34,000 85% of your benefits are taxed.

If you're married and earn under $32,000 in income from other sources your benefits aren't taxed. If you earn between $32- 44,000 half of your Social Security is now subject to taxes. Over $44,000 subjects 85% of your benefits to tax.

For example,e if you're married and you take $40,000 from your IRA and your Social Security is $2,000 per month or $24,000 a year, then $12,000 of your Social Security is now subject to income taxes. Over $44,000 makes $20,400 of you benefits subject to tax.

Pensions and annuities are taxed at ordinary income tax rates. These are the rates you're most familiar with. Once you start the income from pensions, annuities and Social Security you generally can't stop it. You can't take money in one tax year and not another so once you start you need to shift your tax management strategies to other sources of income.

IRAs, 401(k) s and other forms of deferred income are also subject to ordinary income taxes. Except for some non-deductible IRAs, the money you deferred for income tax purposes is now entirely subject to income taxes. It doesn't matter how the money is invested inside the account, you never paid taxes on the contributions or gains and now the entire amount is subject to taxes when you withdraw the funds.

This tax liability needs to be viewed as an overall reduction in your perceived wealth. For example, if you have $500,000 in your 401(k), the IRS has dibs on about a third of it or roughly $150,000 leaving you with $350,000 in actual wealth. You can't take the full $500,000 and spend it. You can earn money on the entire amount but you can't spend it all without paying taxes.

Your personal savings consist of money you earned, paid taxes on and saved. The base level, or principal, remains tax free but depending on how you invested your savings your taxes on withdrawals will be some combination of interest, dividends and capital gains. Capital gains and certain dividends can be taxed at a lower rate than ordinary income tax rates giving you some flexibility to lower the tax bite on money you withdraw.

Finally, you can get tax free money from Municipal bonds, Roth IRAs and when you spend principal. Municipal bonds are bonds issued by state and local governments and most of them are exempt from income taxes. They usually pay a lower amount than standard US Treasury bonds, but if you are in the highest of income tax brackets you may be better off with Municipal bonds.

Roth IRAs required you to convert a standard IRA, pay income taxes and set the balance into a specially designated Roth IRA. Roth IRAs then grow tax free and withdrawals are tax free. If you didn't go through the conversion process then you don't have a Roth IRA. Most people didn't convert to Roth IRAs.

You don't pay taxes on the principal you take from your savings to meet your monthly expenses because you already have paid taxes on it. In retirement you'll have a number of tax pockets from which you can draw income. You'll need to find the most efficient combination.

To figure out the best combination you'll need to decide how much income you want to take, when to take it and from which tax pocket. With these decided you can estimate your tax bill by using the published tax rates.

Tax rates are a bit more complex. In general, the more you make the more you pay in taxes. Also, the more you make the higher the percent of your income is taxed. Part of the game is to keep the percentage in taxes you pay down.

SINGLE TAX PAYER		MARRIED TAX PAYER	
$523,600 + _____	37%	$628,300 _____	37%
$209,425 _____	35%	$418.850 _____	35%
$164,925 _____	32%	$329,850 _____	32%
$ 86,375 _____	24%	$172,750 _____	24%
$ 40,525 _____	22%	$ 81,050 _____	22%
$ 9,950 _____	12%	$ 19,900 _____	12%
Exempt _____	10%	Exempt _____	10%

The tax ladders show the dollar threshold and the percent of taxes above that threshold you will pay. The exempt amount is the standard deduction and is $12,550 for singles and $25,100 for married couples. You begin to pay taxes on the amount above the exempt level up to your total income. Your total income is the income from all taxable sources less your allowable tax deductions.

The ladders are cumulative. That is you pay the percent tax rate times dollar amount in each step. For example, if you're single you would pay 10% on the amount above the exempt level of $12,550 and the next step on the ladder of $9,950. You then pay 12% on the amount above $9,950 up to $40,525 and so on. Then, you add all of the stepped amounts together to get your total tax bill.

The amount of money you take from your tax pockets determines how high you climb the ladder. If you can take money that is not taxable, you can stay on the lower rungs. If you have a year when you need to make a major expense, such as buying a car, the cost of the car bumps you up the ladder and you would pay the taxes on your withdrawal at a higher percentage tax rate thus making the car more costly.

It'll be tough to keep tax efficiency in mind when the storm batters you about and you fervently seek money to meet the unexpected. This is where planning ahead proves its worth. But, as you go through the year there are three strategies to keep in mind:

- **Defer** – when possible avoid taking money from your IRA/401(k). Withdrawals from these accounts are fully taxed and you lower the amount you have in the account that can earn future tax deferred gains. At age 70 ½ you must begin minimum withdrawals. The current minimum is about 3% of the total deferred amount.

- **Timing** – sometime during the last few months of the year you need to review your taxable income, deductions and your likely expense level the following year. If it looks like tax rates will go up next year, take additional income this year. If you have a major expense next year, take some of the money this year and some next year so the total tax is kept to the lowest ladder rung possible.

- **Tax Rates** – you have flexibility in where and when you take income. You should strategically target the highest level of taxes you are comfortable with and stay below that amount. In retirement, you'll need to file quarterly tax estimates with payments so this would be a good time to review where you stand.

- **Taxable Income** - you can incur taxable income even if you don't take the income. For example, income on your CDs or interest earned in your brokerage account is taxable whether or not you withdraw the interest. You should take taxable investment income before you take money out of your IRAs or other deferred sources.

Taxes are likely to be one of your biggest budget expenses. Less money paid in taxes, leaves more to maintain your lifestyle and more to invest in your retirement security. Too many people consider the tax bill something that comes due and must be paid. These people either do their own taxes or get them done and upon completion simply pay what's owed.

You need to take a proactive approach to this large budget item and manage it as you would any other large expense. If you are going to travel extensively, you'll likely come up with a plan and an estimate of its costs. You need to do the same with your taxes.

This exercise should be part of your Expense and Activity Plan. Decisions on taxes can't be done in isolation from your investment decisions and will be further examined in Step 4.

Drawdown Ratio

Many things in life seem to work better when they stay in balance. Diet, exercise, relationships and work are a few. As a new retiree you'll need to keep your income needs and income sources in balance. You don't want to be overly attentive or worried about money. You want to go about living your life knowing you are financially secure.

To keep your retirement viable and sustainable you'll need to know when your income needs and income sources fall out of balance. The coming storm will knock things off the shelf and rearrange your carefully established order. The sooner you know when your expenses or the value of your savings tilt you off balance the quicker you can make adjustments and prepare for the new order.

One measure of the income balance is the Drawdown Ratio. This ratio serves as a warning gauge on your LPOD. A rising rate signals danger while a falling rate signals improved security. The rate measures how fast you're taking money out of your savings to how fast your savings are earning money. If you're taking money faster than it's earning, trouble lies ahead.

The concept of a drawdown rate is discussed more often in the popular press. But it is somewhat misleading and implies a one-size-fits-all approach. It's a static number that doesn't offer warnings when things awry.

The financial experts babble about 4% being the ceiling on your withdrawals. If you stay at or below this level you should be fine. This number is based on the assumption you will earn more than 4% on average over time. That's not an unreasonable assumption.

However, the problem lies in what to do should you earn less than 4% for several consecutive years while you are taking money out of your savings or if you must increase your withdrawals for an extended period of time. Your ratio changes each year. Just because you started your retirement with a rate of 4% or below doesn't mean you're financially secure.

It is how the number changes over time that's important. Simply, the Drawdown Ratio takes the withdrawals from your savings and divides it by the total value of your savings. For example, if you need to take out $2,000 a month, or $24,000 a year and the total value of your savings is $240,000 your drawdown rate is 10%. However, if your total savings is $1 million your drawdown rate is 2.4%.

Your Drawdown Ratio needs context. You might think taking 10% a year out of your savings will drain your savings quickly which is likely. Similarly, you may think taking our 2.4% means your money will last a long time, this is also likely. Together these numbers should give you a feeling of when things are likely to get out of balance.

But, interpreting a safe rate is also dependent on how much you earn on your investments and how old you are. The more you can earn on your investments the more you can take out and the older you are the more you can take out since the money won't need to last as long.

If you're 92, taking out 10% a year shouldn't be a problem. It also is less of a problem if you're an astute investor earning 9% a year on your money. In both cases it's remotely possible each of these characters could run out of money. The safe zone is where you take out less money than you earn. But, this measurement is in constant change and your Drawdown Ratio captures the changes.

To calculate your Drawdown Ratio you start with your total estimate lifestyle expense. Using the previous example:

INCOME NEEDS

Personal Activities	$ 750
Others' Activities	600
Home	2,000
Health	500
Consumer Debt	200
General Living	<u>1,000</u>
Total	$5,050
Income taxes @15%	$ 891
Total Monthly Expense	$5,941
LESS INCOME SOURCES:	
Social Security	$2,500
Pensions	<u>1,500</u>
INCOME FROM SAVINGS	$1,941

In this example you would need to withdraw $1,941 a month from your savings or $23,292 a year. Is this a workable number? It depends on how old you are and how much you have saved.

In this example, the couple is newly retired and they are both 65 years old. They saved $600,000 in IRAs and other personal savings. This gives them a Drawdown Ratio of 3.88%, edgy but doable. They feel they can earn 6% on their savings and if necessary, they can reduce expenses.

If you have yet to retire, your Drawdown Ratio can serve as a guide as to when you can retire with a sense of financial security. The larger your rate, the riskier it is to retire, the smaller the safer. If you are retired, your rate serves as a starting point, one that gives you reference and orients you when things change.

DRAWDOWN SAFE ZONE
6% Investment Return

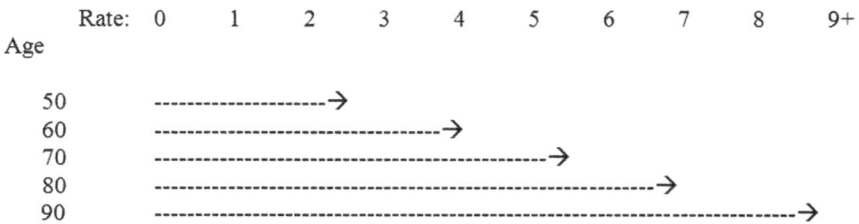

Rate:	0	1	2	3	4	5	6	7	8	9+

Age

```
50    -------------------→
60    ------------------------------------→
70    ----------------------------------------------------→
80    ----------------------------------------------------------------→
90    ------------------------------------------------------------------------------→
```

Implicit in the safe zone is the concept of not spending principal to meet your living expenses. You don't know how long you're going to live and thereby need to have your money last as long as it can. If you limit the money you spend to the money you earn your principal stays in tack and can continue to earn money to meet future needs.

But, as you get older and when the money doesn't need to last as long, you can judiciously eat into principal to maintain your lifestyle and not outlive your money. In the chart above the 90 year-old can use 3% a year in principal to meet lifestyle needs.

At age 95 the principal has been eroded by 15% but there still should be plenty of money. If this person gets a third wind and feels there are many more years ahead, she can always reduce the money being withdrawn.

At earlier ages, taking considerably less than you earn, adds to your financial security. For example, if you are age 50, taking 2.5% and earning 6%, allows you to build up principal to generate more income in the future to offset the effects of inflation. As you age, the money doesn't need to last as long and you can shrink the difference between what you take out and what you earn by increasing your Drawdown Ratio.

Your Drawdown Ratio is a critical gauge on the dashboard of your LPOD. It's a dynamic measurement that captures changes going on around you. It lets you know if you are becoming more financially secure or if there are dangers requiring your attention.

Investment earnings and values will change. How you spend money will change. The relationship of these changes is captured by your Drawdown Ratio. When your ratio begins to get uncomfortably high, the gauge signals you to take a closer look at your spending and investment results. The signal could help you to uncover the culprit before a lot of damage is done.

You may be tempted to feel that the problem can be readily solved by earning more on your investments. This is a possibility but you will need to take on more risk and increase the chance of losing money. The gathering storm will change the investment landscape making it harder to manage risks.

Most of the Western World is broke. The high historical rates of return are less meaningful in the new environment. History will be of less value in guessing how much you can earn on your investments.

Debt will need to be repaid. Taxes will need to be raised slowing the economy and keeping unemployment high. Fewer people working will cause less money to be invested in retirement plans.

The increasing new retiree population will begin cashing in long term investments. Inflation is likely to rebound. All of these together combine to create a strong headwind slowing down investment returns.

It is unlikely during your stay in retirement that you can consistently earn much more than 6%. A more likely range will be 4-5% although you are bound to have years with the occasional double-digit return. Battening down to survive the storm will compel you to take less investment risk. Now is not the time to roll the dice.

Chapter 8

SAVINGS – THE NEW RETIREE PERSPECTIVE
STEP 4B

Your relationship with your savings changes when you retire. While you worked it was a long-distance relationship. You could take the long-term view on its degree of health or dysfunction. Like any relationship, you rode the ups and downs.

When times were good you excitedly checked your savings statements for what seemed to be ever increasing balances. Your confidence in a secure retirement steadily rose with each new statement.

When the tough times came it was excruciatingly hard for you to simply open your statements. You reassured yourself that with patience and time balance would be restored. Now as you near retirement you fear the balance.

If your long-distance relationship is to become a long term relationship your savings needs to move home on the day you retire. You'll look at it differently. It becomes not this outside thing left alone to grow, but rather something requiring regular attention.

In retirement your needs will change and your relationship with your savings will have to change with it. The once continuous flow from your paycheck into your savings gets replaced by the trickle of Social Security. You're now charged with skillfully watering and pruning your savings garden to provide you with immediate and sustainable sustenance.

The paycheck flow disguised how your investments behaved by amplifying market ups and dampening market declines. The true nature of investment performance was distorted. Now you will feel the frequency and magnitude in changes to your wealth n real time.

Accommodations and adjustments must be made for any relationship to thrive. Things that worked in your long term relationship hinder you when practiced in the day-to-day. When viewed up close, unseen characteristics of the object of your desire arise and previously known traits gain clarity.

Your savings is now charged with producing income not accumulating deposits. It shifts attention from increasing the market risks you take to grow your savings to reducing the risks you take to protect your savings.

You need to become nimble and flexible in the management of your wealth. Managing your savings to produce reliable and sustainable income is considerably more complex than managing it for accumulation.

The risks you take must be more calculating and deliberate. You need to be better informed as to where your money takes up residence. You must be able to anticipate and respond to ever changing economic, political and personal changes.

All of this needs to be done in a timely and intelligent manner if your savings are to power your LPOD through the years ahead.

Savings Portfolio

Your savings must be managed to support your overall retirement plan. It shouldn't be a hodgepodge of investments pieced together by some magazine's recommendations or forced into some pie chart you found on a financial web site. Your savings plan must be personalized to you support your overall retirement plan and reflect your current outlook.

Your priorities have changed and you need to realign your resources to meet them. This requires a new strategy and a new way of thinking about how you manage your savings and investments.

You want to avoid becoming a fixed income retiree in a rising cost world. For the fixed income crowd, it simply becomes a matter of time before they notice they are exchanging today's perceived security for tomorrow's vulnerabilities. When you limit your options, you limit your ability to respond.

You need to become a variable income retiree in a rising cost world. Your income should not only be capable of increasing it should also come from multiple sources. If Social Security or your pension gets cut, or you're hit with increased expenses, you need to crank up some other part of your savings to make up the difference.

You can begin to rethink how you will manage your savings by separating it into strategic and tactical components. The strategic is more of the big picture of where you are and where you want to go. The tactical is how you will actually get there.

This can be compared to white water rafting. Your strategic evaluation would include the specific river, the time of the year, water levels among other things and you also might get one of those aerial shots of the portion of the river you want to raft. This evaluation will help you set your overall plan and how you want to proceed.

The tactical portion would include the type of raft, who you are going with, provisions, first aid a compass and so on. You would verify your plan and double check your readiness before you enter the water.

But, a lot can happen. You don't know with certainty what lies ahead. Your strategic plan may have miscalculated the snow melt and the water runoff thus making the river higher and faster.

You may not have prepared adequately for the insects, bears and snakes. You may find yourself uncontrollably speeding down a level 4 river hoping you can steer clear of the rocks and sudden drops.

When you put your savings at risk you will find times when its value seems to take off on its own. Your ability to direct it will be restricted. You may find you want to do something but simply can't.

To avoid losing control and to retain the ability to manage your savings you will need to make a clear-headed assessment of the risks you are willing to take on. You make better decisions when you articulate your goals.

Strategic Goals
• Inflation-protected income
• Minimize Losses
• Manageable Drawdown Ratio

At the strategic level you decide where you'll park your savings. Basically, you can divide your savings among cash, bonds, stocks and real assets. Each has a particular set of benefits and risk characteristics. The strategic challenge is to allocate your savings in such a way that you gain the benefits while minimizing your risks.

The total of those decisions becomes your portfolio design, your asset allocation. Once your strategy is in place it can't simply sit still. The storm will continually disrupt your savings balances and shift levels of risk. Your strategy will need to adjust to changing circumstances just like you would change your approach in a sports game against a worthy opponent who altered his game.

When you worked, you not only got a paycheck you also likely received cost-of-living increases. It may be clearer in your mind that you need to replace a portion of your paycheck than is the value of those annual pay increases.

The coming storm will shift new costs to you and raise the cost of your everyday purchases. The government is likely to use inflation as one tool to reduce its massive debt. To keep up your lifestyle your savings will need to generate ever increasing income.

Another cause of rising costs will be the decline in the value of the US dollar. In a globally connected world, the dollar decline will add an extra boost to your cost-of-living as goods from abroad cost more. You'll get doubly squeezed by rising costs and lowering purchasing power.

Experience has taught you about market losses. To minimize losses, you need to know where you started and where you are. You may invest in something that goes down in value. At some point you decide to bail out or ride it out. Here your thinking is mostly on the principal value of what you invested.

Something more subtle and equally important is the reduction in accumulated investment gains. When you continue to hold an investment with accumulated gains these too can be subject to declines. In the scheme of your portfolio watching gains dissipate can be as painful as watching principal erode.

Giving up gains follows a different thought process than losing principal as there are tax consequences. Both affect how you make strategic adjustments to your savings allocations. Both reduce the total wealth you have available to produce income.

Your Drawdown Ratio can rise from both your savings and your expenses. If your savings earn less than what you planned to earn your ratio rises. If your expenses exceed your budget your ratio rises.

A rising Drawdown Ratio is manageable in the short term but becomes a critical indicator of future problems if left unchecked.

Your strategy sets the big picture but how you go about putting into action is equally important. Mistakes at the tactical level can be as disruptive as mistakes at the strategic level.

Tactical Goals
- Decision maker
- Selection process
- Flexibility

All sorts of things can go wrong during the implementation and management of your savings. Tactical risks center on who makes the decision, how decisions are made and how easily you can change course.

You need to decide up front if you will make the investment decisions or if you will work with an advisor. If you'll be making the decisions you need to be clear on how you will go about making, monitoring and changing your decisions to reflect disruptions from the storm.

You'll need to follow a due diligence process if you're going to work with an advisor. It's important to know how the advisor is paid and whether there are conflicts-of-interest. You'll also need to make clear your expectations.

The selection process works better when the information available is complete, objective and trustworthy. Much of the information you get comes with a sales bias. Much of the advice in the popular media is directed towards the average investor with over-simplified assumptions.

These sources can be a good starting point but more hard work is required if you are to tailor the information and advice to your particular needs. You'll also need to have a method to compare and contrast different investments to see how they fit together to support your overall strategic plan.

The storm will be disruptive. What's there at one point in time may be different later. You'll need to have built in flexibility in your plan. Some investments may lock you in for a long period of time. Others may charge you early withdrawal penalties if you take your money out before some designated date.

Some investments need to be held for a period of time if you are to mitigate the risks and gain the benefits. If some portion is locked up, other parts of your portfolio need to be capable of quick cost-free changes when you need to respond to the unexpected.

The benefits of particular investments will need to be aligned with your retirement needs. In a sense, each investment will be assigned a role; each will have a purpose. It will perform some specific task. The collection of your savings and investments will no longer be solely geared towards growing wealth but to generate income and protect principal.

Investment Risk

Investment risk is different than other retirement risks. The other risks, like health, disability, and loss of loved ones tend to be driven by their own set of forces. Those forces seem to be more complex and not fully understood. Where possible, you avoid the associated risks and when you can't it simply is better to be prepared.

Investment risk, the chance of reduced lifestyle, is something you initiate. You willingly choose to take on risk by deciding how and where you invest your money. Investment risk tends to be guided by a set of man-made rules which regularly are mocked by things out there that don't play by the rules.

You're a better investor when you understand the rules and the outside influences. There are some risks that can be managed and reduced while others risks are simply unpredictable. If those other retirement risks are best avoided, why would you willingly take on investment risk?

You wouldn't if you had more than enough in savings to cover and maintain your lifestyle. If you had $15 million in savings and only needed $100,000 a year to maintain your lifestyle you could avoid risk by investing all of your money in short term insured government bonds.

Similarly, if your wealth and lifestyle were in balance at a more modest level, you might be able to leave your savings in the bank invested in insured CDs.

You would take on the risk if what you can earn on your savings is not enough to meet your expenses today and cover inflation tomorrow. You are induced into taking on investment risk when the risk of doing nothing is greater than doing something. Yet, there are prudent ways and reckless ways to take on investment risk.

When you begin to compare your living expenses with your savings, you'll feel the push and pull of investment risk. In a low interest rate environment, like the period 2009-2011 when short term interest rates were less than 1%, you can't earn enough interest off your savings to cover your living costs.

If you do nothing you are confronted with eating into your principal and running out of money or lowering your lifestyle. This agitated mental state pushes you to take on more investment risk to have a chance to grow your principal to increase your income to cover your monthly expenses.

The pull of investment risk lures you out of your safe zone with the temptation of making more money. You might come across an investment offering you 8% interest. This amount greatly exceeds your Drawdown Ratio and could set you up for years of financial security.

But, what's the catch? The general bias when investing is the interest rate or the potential return on your investment is readily quantifiable while the risk is not. You can relate to 8% and it seems more real than the risk associated with the investment.

You would assess the risk differently on the 8% investment if the offering was from a large established company rather than from your brother-in-law who wants to start a cupcake factory.

You may realize that the key risks you're taking on include actually getting paid the 8% and getting your money back in a timely fashion. But these risks are not easily quantifiable.

The decision-making part of your brain begins to balance your fear with greed. Depending on which wins, you make your investment choice. What tends to get overlooked is the voice screaming outside your window why anyone would pay you 8% in a 1% interest rate environment.

In the financial markets there is a relationship between risk and return. You are enticed by a higher rate of return when you take on higher risk. Though remember, there is no guarantee of getting a higher return simply because you've taken on higher risk.

Some risks you take on you get a chance of getting a higher return if there is underlying economic value. For example, if you choose to invest in an individual company, you take the risk the company won't go out of business or suffer setbacks or the economy won't slip into recession. In return for your patience, you get the chance of participating in future profits and growth of the company.

Other risk you take on, if there is no substantive economic value, the chance of a higher return is purely speculative. If you day trade, you take on the risk of the market's ups and downs. Since there is no underlying economic value being created, this type of risk is pure speculation. Playing the movements of the markets is simply gambling.

An underlying risk all investors take on is the risk in the financial system itself. When banks teeter on default or cash availability and credit dry-up, all assets suffer. Similarly, changes in politics, taxes and the overall economy create a separate set of risks.

The financial experts make it seem investment risk is readily manageable. It's made to seem that if you just wait long enough and spread your money around risk disappears over time. It hasn't worked out that way over the last twenty years.

There were market crashes in 1987 when the market lost 25% in one day; in 1997 when Long Term Capital Management collapsed during the ruble and Asian currency crises; in 2000 at the end of the dot com boom, in 2001 with 9/11 and in 2008 with the mortgage mess. Followed by 2020 COVID crash.

Holding steady and true did not increase wealth much less preserve it. You lost money, probably a lot. You allocated and diversified your assets. You held your positions for the long term. What happened to all of these risk management tools and techniques that were supposed to protect you?

In the early days, risk was considered managed if you made investment decisions as a 'prudent man' would. This led to the 'Prudent Man' Rule. Courts used it as a guide for trustees as a safe harbor when overseeing money on another person's behalf.

Prudence dictated investments should be made for income with as little risk to principal as possible. There was less emphasis on investing for price appreciation and certainly no speculation. Prudent investors relied on rules-of-thumb, experience, anecdotes and the character of those with whom they invested for guidance.

Times have changes. Instead of prudence we now have statistics. Modern Portfolio Theory (MPT) replaced the 'Prudent Man' rule with statistical analysis. Advocates argued MPT could manage capital asset risk thereby allowing trustees to manage funds for total return that is income and price appreciation.

MPT would cover the downside risk as long as everyone followed its process. MPT placed risk and return into mathematical formulas. Statistical manipulation and forecasting became its forte. It was now was possible for anyone to get an optimal investment portfolio with just the right amount of risk and return.

This became the efficient way to invest. Your target was to be either on the Efficient Frontier or above it. Investing in stocks and similar risky assets was no longer considered speculation as its risk could be managed. You now had a mathematical path to getting higher returns with less risk. Everyone loved it and the bulls ran on Wall Street.

The love fest led to it receiving the Nobel Price in economics. This gave MPT and its spin offs the credibility to seep into the highest reaches of investment and financial management.

The Laureates were celebrated for ushering a new age of finance. No longer did managers have to rely on rules of thumb and experience. The financial wizards and financial rocket scientists took over.

Wall Street issued a slew of new financial products and derivatives in the frenzy to be the first to the market. Billions were made. With easy money to be made, the Laureates drank the kool-aid and took a leave from academia to form a hedge fund known as Long Term Capital Management (LTCM).

Essentially, they took advantage of minute pricing irregularities in the Treasury market and leveraged it to high heaven. After all, they were managing the risk what could go wrong?

In their statistical and random bell curve world, the chance of things happening outside their risk parameters was negligible so they were ignored. Investors flocked to the fund with billions. The fund made money for awhile and high fives and back slaps showed what MPT and its offspring could do.

It also showed what they couldn't do. A crisis erupted in Russia. Its currency plummeted. The markets got nervous about a variety of currencies throughout the world. The emerging markets in Asia and their currencies got whacked.

World interest rates shot up. The value of the bonds held by LTCM nosedived. They no longer had adequate collateral for the billions of debt they took on. This required a major bailout of Wall Street.

Fortunately for taxpayers, this time the bailout was done by Wall Street. Several major firms at the prodding of the Secretary of Treasury ponied up several hundreds of millions of dollars each to repay investors.

We now move to the mortgage mess in 2008. Since statistical risk was perceived to be manageable all sorts of new financial products flooded the investment world in the beginning of the new millennium.

Derivatives, agreements whose values were derived from actual assets, spread like viruses throughout the system. The most famous were real estate mortgages packaged into something called Collateral Debt Obligations (CDO) and Collateralized Mortgage Obligations (CMO). Mortgages were sliced and diced and wrapped in pretty packages and sold to investors, including banks and pension funds.

The risks were managed by the best and brightest on Wall Street. Many banks borrowed up to 50 times their capital base to juice up returns. After all, these institutions had risk management departments. Surely, these would be the people who could manage risk. They were the smartest and had all of the latest tools.

They bought insurance to protect their risks. Since the risks were perceived to be negligible, the insurance cost was relatively cheap. AIG sold a lot of insurance. They made a lot of money. Those insured thought they got a great deal as they new they had more risk than what was being priced into the insurance. Risk was covered.

As long as the markets were rising, that is. Fortunes were made and outsized bonuses given to the top people. It all worked until some astute buyers of the CDOs questioned how these things were valued.

Buyers stopped buying. Markets went down. The financial system neared collapse. Massive taxpayer bailouts prevented the collapse of the financial system at the cost of trillions to individual and institutional investors in lost wealth.

A saying resurfaced during the crises that once the tide goes out you find out who is not wearing a swimsuit. The falling markets showed who was naked and taxpayers paid to cover them up.

Why wasn't this risk managed? Surely it wasn't the caliber of the people. They thought they were doing Yeomen's work. This leads to questioning the theories, models and practices. Or, to realizing there is something out there that simply is unpredictable and unmanageable.

Yet through all of these crises MPT theory lives on. At its core it uses *future* estimates of average returns, standard deviations and correlations. It also assumed that investments results are random and fit into bell curves. This let everyone believe the resulting probabilities could be relied upon. Now you could guess and manage the future.

If these assumption holds than all of the elegant math and statistical analysis makes sense. The follow-on reasoning is solid but it may be derived from a false premise.

Assume pigs can fly. Then it would be reasonable for you to buy steel reinforced umbrellas and for the government to mandate helmets for pedestrians under age 15. It would also be reasonable to clear areas for the pigs to land and take off and clearly reasonable to keep the flying pigs away from airports, that is, if pigs could fly.

Investment results can be viewed as random when viewed from satellite distances. Once you zoom in you find investments are markets and people make up the markets. Most people don't make their decisions randomly. It can get quite messy at times.

You probably never woke up one morning with the uncontrollable urge to put all of your savings into Guatemalan Taco franchises. Similarly, a professional trader does not decide to wager $1 billion of the firm's capital on the Thai Baht because he had good take out.

Yet when looked at as historical data, the collective decision making can be seen as random. Changes in the market price are relatively small, one-half of one percent or so, and mostly fit within a reasonable range around the average change. This lets most of the data fit into a bell-shaped curve.

Suddenly, all of the statistic analysis around averages and the probability calculations from random data seem plausible. Couple this perceived randomness with the hypothesis that the markets are efficient and you have the base view of MPT.

If things were random you wouldn't have outsized market changes like the five huge market drops in the last 20 years. Statistically, this would be near impossible to happen and consequently the models ignore this risk. It's something that the models say can't happen.

But when you opened your statements you realized something indeed did happen. You lost a lot of money. MPT says take the long view and these aberrations will average out over time. This gives them the out that they are always right, you just have to wait long enough to see this.

As a new retiree you don't have the luxury to take this long view. Since you will be taking money out of your savings you will most likely experience non-recoverable losses when withdrawals are coupled with market declines.

The next key premise is the 'Efficient Market' hypothesis. This claims everyone in the market has access to all available information and everyone has the level of skills to analyze the information and make dispassionate decisions; that investors are rational.

Have you ever seen a trading pit portrayed in a movie or seen market valuation bubbles like dot.com companies?

People make decisions from gathering and assessing information. Most apply their personal experience to the mix. Since they lack perfect information they need to do some guessing. Herein lay the emotions, intuition and other things that are not clearly rational. Their decisions in turn affect results and information out there requiring new assessments and new decisions.

This makes the data points in the models interactive. When one data agent can affect another data agent you don't have characteristics of a group of random data. This is like saying your height impacts the height of those around you and people get shorter or taller when they are in your presence.

Efficient markets hypothesis states since you can't predict future market values from historical data markets must be efficient. Yet most predictive models used by financial advisors use historical data to project the future. Times change, historical data don't.

If markets are random and efficient why pay anyone to make investment decisions for you? You wouldn't if you are an advocate of this line of thinking. Instead you would simply buy unmanaged index funds.

But it is important to know the difference between something that is unpredictable with something that is random. Just because something is unpredictable doesn't mean it's random. Markets are unpredictable but in the short term they are not random.

Investment markets also are assumed to be closed systems lending themselves to probabilistic predictions. You can make guesses about the future using probabilities as a guide if there is no outside interference.

In closed systems, games being representative, probabilities or odds or chances can be calculated with confidence. If you flip a coin you have a 50/50 chance of getting a head or a tail. You know the odds of a roulette table. The odds don't change as you play the game.

With investments it's not so simple. Economists can't tell you what GNP will be next quarter or next year much less the 30 years showing Social Security is properly funded. They will site probabilities to justify their forecasts. It is jokingly reported that economists have predicted six of the last three recessions.

These predictions are mostly and consistently wrong yet they are regularly followed. These at best are educated guesses and need to be understood as such. Just because math is involved and results come from a computer doesn't change the nature of them being guesses.

If markets are unpredictable then you don't know the probability of any future event. You can't play the odds if you don't know them. But when you look at all of those models on retirement web sites, this is precisely what they are doing.

They take average returns and statistical probability risk to determine whether you have enough money to make it through retirement. These projections go well out into the future and you are confidently presented with an investment strategy based on those averages and probabilities.

It is interesting to compare those projections with the regulatory requirement that any published investment result must contain a disclosure that past performance is not indicative of future performance.

You can be equally accurate in predicting the weather by saying tomorrow will be like today. You will be right more times than wrong.

hat if tomorrow brings a tornado or hurricane? The statistical models never predict large variations or a sudden change in direction.

The retirement storm will batter things about. Results won't be driven by past data observations. Results will come from many people making many decisions. Fear and greed drive the market for short bursts of time. They are neither efficient, rational nor random.

As a retiree you need to place greater emphasis on the near term if you are to protect your wealth from large swings in value. You need to pay attention to what is happening around you and make changes when warranted.

You can't take the chance of suffering a huge market loss because some theory tells you these are near impossible events. Nor can you make an investment today and forget about it thinking you have the reassurance if held for the long term you will make money.

To manage the uncertainty of investing you will need to bring back some of the sensibilities of the prudent investor and compliment those sensibilities with rational analysis. You shouldn't take comfort in the statistical fact that you, on average, are safe.

Managing Investment Uncertainty

Sitting in principal protected savings seems safe and secure. Until you begin to realize the interest you are being paid is not enough to supplement your Social Security and pensions to maintain your lifestyle. You now must choose a lower lifestyle or an increased level of investment risk.

When you open your saving account statement you get an initial sense of security to see your balance rising; however slight the rise. The rising balance deludes you into thinking your overall wealth has increased. But, the ultimate test of the value of your wealth is what it can buy. Unfortunately, your statements don't tell you the purchasing power of your safe and secure savings.

Inflation stealthily erodes wealth. Your savings balance may have increased but what you can buy with your savings has decreased. This can be maintained for short periods of time. If left unchecked, later in life you may find yourself choosing between food and medicine.

Pressure on your monthly budget makes you realize you need to move some of your nest egg from your safe lair into the uncertain world of investments where wealth is created and destroyed. You can stay safe and potentially starve or move forward where you have a chance to thrive.

Moving forward you will find an overwhelming number of investment choices. For example, there are over 4,500 mutual funds and that's just one type of investment. Then consider all of these investment choices are in an environment of uncertainty. Now add in the consequences of bad decisions and you find any decision become daunting.

To get your mind around all of this is enormously complex. No wonder many people opt to be lulled by simplistic statistical solutions and hope for the best. Once retired, you no longer can afford the side effects of these models. What can you do instead?

When faced with something massively complex and uncertain it is rather sensible to use a few simple rules for guidance. These rules can help clear the immediate clutter and provide a limited view of what lies ahead.

The rules help you take action and exert some control over your wealth. If you stay flexible and nimble you can avoid severe setbacks while you intelligently steward your wealth.

There are four practices you can apply when making investment decisions in an uncertain environment. These practices may be familiar but need to be viewed differently as a retiree.

Remember as a new retiree your primary focus is to preserve wealth and generate income, not beat the market or make as much money as you can. These practices won't help you avoid all losses, but they will lessen the chances of losing a lot of money.

Cash and Money Markets

Cash and money market investments include checking, savings, money market funds, Treasury Bills and other short-term debt with a maturity of less than one year. They minimize the chances for principal loss and pay you a small amount of interest.

These are the investments you use when you think of safety. This group should be used more frequently in your overall investment plan to protect against disruptions caused by the coming storm. The storm will place renewed stress on the financial system and economies around the world. This can be your safe harbor a place to ride our periods of turbulence.

Moving your money from a risk asset to cash or a safe asset is derided as market timing. Many studies show market timing doesn't work. The major problem with these studies is they focus on the rate of return comparing market timing to holding pat.

What they don't explore is the lower risk position you've taken. In the immediacy of the now shedding risk may be the most prudent thing you can do. Your new perspective as a retiree is to preserve principal not take the chance that on average if you hold your positions you will be made whole. A lot can go wrong during the wait.

Yet, safety isn't guaranteed. You need to be aware of some caveats. Banks can fail. Although you may be covered by FDIC insurance, it is limited to a specific dollar amount. In the last financial crisis the amount was temporarily increased to $250,000 per account but is scheduled to drop back to $100,000 per account. Even if you are covered by insurance there still may be considerable delays in gaining access to your money should your bank fail.

Money markets have an industry agreement to keep the value of the funds at $1 per share. The price stays fixed but the interest credited varies. This keeps your principal secure. Nonetheless, the $1 is a voluntary agreement. One large fund couldn't maintain the $1 threshold when Lehman brothers collapsed in the financial mess and defaulted on its debt.

The fund went out of business but was bought out by other industry participants. They kept the promise of $1 in order to maintain trust among investors and prevent a run on all of the other money markets. This should serve as a warning in the next financial mess holdings here may be less safe than presumed.

Treasury bills may be the last bastion of safety should the storm threaten an already weakened financial system. The US government guarantees these and has a printing press to back it up.

If you have large amounts of money that needs to be kept protected when chaos strikes the financial world Treasury Bills are where you want to be. You can buy these directly from the Federal Reserve without cost or through most banks and brokerage companies.

Asset Allocation

Asset allocation is simply investing your money into a number of different asset classes. This is a way to spread your wealth and not leave you too concentrated in one investment where an unexpected event causes you large losses. Asset allocation is most familiar by ubiquitous pie charts in the financial media portioning slices to different asset classes.

The primary asset classes should be considered in global terms, not solely US include:

- Cash
- Short term bonds
- Long term bonds
- Stocks
- Real assets, real estate, homes, businesses
- Precious metals
- Commodities

Most investments out there are some version of these asset classes. The classes respond differently to financial and economic changes. For a given change, one class may do better than expected while a different class does worse. Overall, asset allocation should provide a degree of stability to the value of your investments. You forego large ups in order to reduce the chance of large downs in your savings.

The classes may respond differently at times yet they all are linked through the globalization of the economy. Each is affected by interest rates and credit availability. This is why asset allocation didn't prevent losses during the financial crises when markets worldwide collapsed.

Asset allocation, except for Treasury Bills, does not protect you when the system is stressed and near collapse. If all markets everywhere go down, asset allocation won't prevent from losing money. Only your foresight and action provide protection.

Asset allocation does allow you to adjust your exposure to risk and uncertainty and this determines how much you can potentially lose. If your outlook changes, you can change the amount of dollars you have in each asset class. For instance, if you think interest rates will rise, you can shift some of the dollars from bonds to stocks.

If you want to reduce overall market risk you can move money from the markets into cash investments to ride out periods of volatility. Once your funds are allocated, you can adjust the dial on how much money is given to each asset class to reflect your view of the world economy.

You don't need to stay on for the wild roller coaster ride of past years. You can step aside and take a breather now and then.

Diversification

Diversification further spreads your wealth among additional investments within each asset class. For example, the money you allocate to stocks shouldn't all be in one company. You would spread that money to a number of companies to continue to reduce risk. This acts like a stabilizing base for your savings.

Like Asset Allocation, diversification doesn't help you avoid losses. If the overall market goes down, so will your investments in the market regardless of how well you have diversified.

Where diversification helps you is to spread risks facing specific companies or industries. This prevents you from having too much of your money in one place that suffers large losses.

Enron and WorldCom were accounting frauds and went bankrupt. Lehman Brothers took on too much financial risk and went bankrupt. BP had an oil spill and lost nearly half of its value. Greek bonds neared default and people rioted in the streets. When all of your money is concentrated in one or two investments you can lose a lot of money.

Each stock and debt issuer brings its own set of investment risk. The same is true for real estate and commodities. Companies have management risk, lawsuit exposures and a number of particular business risks in addition to market risk. Debt issuers have credit ratings that could change and their ability to meet interest payments could get strained.

Real estate and commodities can be affected by interest rate changes and credit availability and whether the economy is growing or slowing down. The risks that are particular to a specific investment can be diversified away by holding different investments in the same asset class.

If the value of one investment goes down for a particular reason, you entire asset class does not need to suffer the same fate. Spreading your money around may prevent you from hitting the home run but should also prevent your from striking out.

Holding Periods

Most investors were educated to hold investments for the long term because the market always comes back. They were also informed that they couldn't time the market so why try. This led many people to shovel money into their 401(k) s and watch its value deteriorate over the following decade.

An old story exemplifies the dangers of assuming the future will be like the past. There was a turkey who was thrilled every morning and afternoon as the farmer came in to feed it and clean its space. This was going of for what seemed to the turkey to be forever.

The turkey began to anticipate the arrival of the farmer. Like clockwork, the turkey was fed and its space cleaned. It was a comfortable life. The turkey gained weight and didn't have to worry about predators. Overall, it seemed like a good life.

Then one morning in mid November the farmer came with a determined look on his face. He did not bring any food. The turkey sensed something was wrong but didn't know what to do. After countless days of being fed and cleaned, it now appeared the turkey's true role of being the star of Thanksgiving was revealed.

You were conditioned to buy and hold mutual funds, stocks and other investments for the long term. The curious thing is that the mutual fund and separate account managers buy and sell stocks daily. They rarely hold investments for the long term and in most cases not even for a year. What do they know that you don't? What is your true role?

Complacency has its costs. If you simply buy and hold your investments while taking money out of your savings your wealth can evaporate quickly. For example, if you split your money 50/50 between stocks and bonds and took out the $24,000 a year in from our example here is what happens to the value of your principal for the years 1999-2009:

You can't afford to watch your wealth evaporate while you are withdrawing money. The decline becomes precipitous. Yet, investing and taking on risk requires time and patience if you are to get positive returns. As a new retiree you need to take a different approach when investing for extended periods of time.

You don't have the ability to take on large losses. You also don't have the time and replenishing paychecks to make them up. To take on investment risk to get higher returns you will need to harvest gains and cut losses.

This can be guided by trading bands. For example, when an investment is up 10% consider selling it and taking your gains. On the down side, you may place a 5% band on losses. When an investment hits the 5% limit it should be brought to your attention to see if it should be sold.

The world around you will continue to change. The coming storm will exacerbate the change in unknown ways. Your money management skills will be tested. To pass the test you will need to anticipate coming change and respond intelligently.

Chapter 9

SAVINGS – PURPOSEFUL INVESTING STEP 4B

Old retirees were able to take a simpler approach to investing. Their Social Security was more secure and medical costs were relatively contained. Overall inflation was low. The expense side of their retirement was more predictable and perceived to be easier to control.

The US was the most dominating economy in the world. The dollar was strong. Government debt was manageable. This created a stable environment for retirees to invest their savings.

Back then, most retirees opted to put 70-80% of their savings into government bonds or CDs. The balance was invested in dividend paying blue chip stocks to provide some additional income and growth. Old retirees' expenses and investments were generally stable and predictable. This made retirement life easier to manage.

When the outside forces rattled expenses and volatility shakes up their predictable interest and dividends old retirees got squeezed. Their choice became one of lowering their lifestyle or invading principal pushing inevitability down the road.

The storm has disrupted both the expense and investment sides of retired life for new retirees. Neither side has much stability. There is greater uncertainty, more volatility and an increased perception of vulnerability. It makes your job of balancing income and expenses to manage your retirement much more difficult.

New retirees have more experience with stocks, bonds and international investments. They are less likely to invest as conservatively as their predecessors. Their higher lifestyle expense requires higher levels of investment risk.

To manage the risk, many followed simple pie chart allocations. This resulted into being labeled conservative, moderate or aggressive. The distinction offered little substance and was simply a matter of how much of your money you invested in stocks.

They became a 60/40 person or some such stock/bond split. At some point many people began to wonder if this was truly a sensible way to part with their savings. The results from the last decade showed the flaws in this approach.

Then the statistical 'gee whiz' kids came along. They were able to dazzle prospects with the probability of making or losing money. Their lexicon of standard deviations, alphas, betas and r squared made it appear that something sophisticated and compelling was being done. New wave asset allocation with its correlations became the mantra.

This approach also did not fare well in the last decade. All of the statistical analysis was based on historical numbers that were assumed to be random. That is, it follows the Bell Curve. Many academic studies show you can't predict future market values from past results.

Yet, that's precisely how all of those models on the web sites and from most financial advisors' work. You are investing your money today based on how the world looked yesterday assuming everything that happened in the past happened randomly.

There is a sense among financial advisors of a need to do something even if what they do is highly flawed. Investors seem to get some comfort from somebody doing something. The mathematical models and analysis seem to offer a higher level of comfort than expert advisors simply giving you their best guesses of what lies ahead.

Some advisors offer predictions based on probability with all the seriousness of high priests. They are rarely wrong. All you have to do is wait long enough and their predictions will come true; if you don't crash and burn in between. It's all average driven. That is, the models assume given enough time things revert to the average.

Averages are tricky things. The average temperature in Chicago is sixty degrees. This bit of knowledge is useless should you arrive at O'Hare airport in the middle of January. If you are six feet tall you should be able to walk across a river that is on average four feet deep.

The critical underlying assumption about averages is you have enough time or events to validate its predictive powers. You can take a quarter and flip it. You have an equal chance of getting a head or a tail. But, if you flip it ten times, you most likely will not get five heads and five tails. Studies show you need to flip it close to a thousand times to get a fifty/fifty result.

As a retiree you may have only a couple of hundred flips left. You can't wait the full time period so you can get the average rate of return. Investing models use averages and long time periods to justify allocation results. These models tend to fall apart when you account for taking money out of your savings.

If you don't have enough time left and you're taking money out of your savings, these models don't live up to their hype. Their sense of control and protection is a delusion sprinkled with statistical fairy dust.

Another flaw in the statistical based models and their analyses is it doesn't tell you how to respond to some pending change in the world around you. This is like watching your house burn down. When its finished burning they can tell you the burn rate and the probability of your house burning down again. Instead, you just want to get the hose and call the fire department.

These approaches are antiseptic. They don't give you a feel or a sense of how your money is working or if it's in danger. You lose the feel of the impact of pending change on your lifestyle.

The storm requires you to have your hands on the helm constantly aware of your surroundings. You need a sort of situational awareness to deftly maneuver through the carnage.

An alternative way to manage your savings is through *Purposeful Investing*. This approach has you target a part of your savings to meet a specific purpose of your overall investment plan. For example, you would assign some of your savings to be next year's income.

Another chunk of money could be set aside to counter the effects of inflation. Additional money can be geared to meet longevity risk or to provide principal growth when the economy is a recovery mode.

As your needs change the purpose of your money changes and you can readily reassign your savings to support your new needs. If something threatens from the outside, like inflation comes roaring back, you can review your inflation position to see if it's still adequate.

Your Drawdown Ratio keeps you connected to short term changes in your income needs and sources. Purposeful Investing empowers you to continually align your long-term resources to your long term needs. It's the protective shadow of your retirement.

New Investment Perspective

Sitting still and doing nothing leaves the value of your savings up to the whims economic, political and financial forces. Moving forward into the fog of uncertainty carries risk and you might suffer losses. But, moving forward gives you a chance to protect and grow your savings to ensure a dignified retirement.

To position your savings requires you to guess about the future. You can make the guesses or pay a financial advisor to make guesses for you. Implied in any guess is the potential to be wrong. Nonetheless, success can be achieved if you are right more often than you are wrong.

One way to provide structure to your investment guesses is to think of investing as a three- story building. On the first floor are the fundamentals of your investments. For example, the bonds you select should provide competitive interest rates with comparable credit quality. Stocks should have profits, growth and good management. Each investment should have economic fundamentals that support its value.

The second floor is where trends reside. Here you will sense if interest rates are rising or falling; inflation is roaring back; the economy is headed into another recession; the dollar is rising or falling or taxes are increasing. These and other broad factors can affect the value of your savings for the near term suggesting you need to alter your investment positions.

The casino is on the third floor. This is where the day traders, computer program trading, hedge funds and speculators and social media warriors reside.

You generally do not want to go to the third floor. This is where the froth and swill of the market seethes. Rallies and corrections get amplified here. The value of your savings whipsaws. The decisions you make in the froth and swill are dangerous.

The first floor is where you use economic fundamentals to support your decisions. This is where risk and return are most closely related. Your strategic and tactical tools help you manage the risk. The fundamentals give you support to hold these positions for longer periods of time. Time and compounding create real wealth.

Yet the world will change and change investment fundamentals. This makes it important for you to take the escalator up to the second floor on occasion and take a look around to see what is changing. The changing world may require you to make changes to your investments; to adjust your asset allocation.

Your investments behave differently when interest rates are rising. Inflation impacts different investments differently. The massive debt loads of the US government increases the risk to the overall economy and changes how markets value things. Economic growth or recession, political upheaval and tax changes also affect values.

Anticipating potential change and allocating your assets accordingly helps you steer your way through the storm debris. Asset allocation acts as a dial on your portfolio. You can tune your exposure to risk to match your tolerance in unsettling environments.

If you must visit the third floor, limit yourself to no more than five percent of your savings. This is the part of the market most associated with gambling. But, instead of Las Vegas odds you are playing with off street bookies. The odds aren't known, the games are stacked against you and the losses can be severe.

Strategic Portfolio Design

Your strategic goals serve as your guide on how you'll allocate your savings. These goals set your personal risk/return balance:

- Inflation-protected income
- Principal preservation
- Managed Drawdown Ratio

Your savings need to supplement your Social Security and pension if you are to live your chosen lifestyle. This requires your savings to produce reliable and sustainable income. To achieve reliable and sustainable income your investments need to support the goals you have set for your retirement.

Your income needs to be predictable; something you can count on. It's better to have your income coming from multiple sources than a single source. This helps you avoid lifestyle disruptions should your sole source of income run into problems.

Your income needs to be sustainable. It needs to be there over the course of your retirement. Over time, inflation will increase your cost of living. Your income needs to support the changing needs of your lifestyle as you go through the Stages of Retirement. It needs to keep pace if you are to avoid the threat of running out of money.

In retirement, your investment focus needs to shift from getting the highest rate of return to getting returns that exceed your Drawdown Ratio. This lessens the chances of losing money. When investment returns exceed your Drawdown Ratio your principal increases over time. Rising principal generates more future income helping you to sustain your lifestyle.

But growth of principal must be balanced by protection of principal. The importance of this balance gets amplified when the storm wreaks volatility on the value of your savings. You'll need to keep reminding yourself that you no longer have a paycheck as a fail safe.

You'll need to be actively involved in how your savings are invested to keep your risk/return in balance. Moving money from risk to safety and back again will be an acquired skill. Learning this skill will help you survive the storm.

As there are simplified rules to manage investment risk, there also are simplified rules to target desired returns for your savings. In the world of investment uncertainty, you need some form of guidance to help you invest in a way that increases the likelihood you'll earn a return greater than your Drawdown Ratio.

To take investment risk you would want the chance of getting a greater return than you would if you kept your money in a bank deposit. Essentially, there are four things you can do with your money: keep it in cash; loan it; invest in a business; or speculate.

There is a fundamental relationship between risk and return. When you keep your money in cash you take little risk. Consequently, you get little return. If, for example, you loan somebody money for one month, you might expect to get your money back and something extra for your time and trouble.

If you were to loan the same person money for one year, you would expect to get a higher return than you would for loaning money for one month. The extra time increases the chance of you not getting paid interest or your principal back. You require a greater return for the greater risk you're taking on.

Similarly, instead of loaning money, you can invest in someone's business. Now you not only have the risk of getting your money back with some return, you now are taking on all of the associated business risk.

It's not just a fulfillment of a promise to repay your investment. Here you actually can lose your entire investment and its part of the deal. You forego recourse. For this level of risk. you would want to a chance to earn a higher return than loaning money.

The further your money moves from you the more things are beyond your control that can go wrong. You would expect the chance of getting a greater return if you are to part with your money long and far.

Investing is similar. Instead of individuals, you might loan money to Governments, corporations or other entities. You might invest in stocks of established companies or in commercial real estate.

You might speculate in commodities or start-up businesses. Each carries its own risk and you would have expectations of what you can earn to entice you to part with your savings.

What you can expect as a return varies not only with specific risk, but also with what is going on in the economy and the political world. Interest rates, inflation, bull markets and bear markets constantly change the perception of value. You need some sort of guidance to spread your savings around in a changing world.

Interest rates can serve as your guide. It's one light through the fog of uncertainty. Interest rates represent the cumulative guesswork of investors of where the economy is and where it's going. They also are manipulated by the Federal Reserve when it wishes to signal its intent to the markets.

Generally, short term rates are lower than long term rates. Rates are made up of credit availability, inflation expectations and bank mark ups. Watching what interest rates do may be the best overall indicator of what is likely to happen to your investments.

Other investments are linked to interest rates. Interest rates are part of the discount rate used to value stocks. Most real estate is financed. Interest rates influence what a purchaser is willing to pay for a property. They influence currency values and gold and commodities as they affect the opportunity cost of holding them.

You can use interest rates as an anchor to estimate the return you can expect from investing in different asset classes. Rates coupled with growth in the economy can serve as a starting point to help you set your investment plan for the coming year.

A prudent investor would use interest rates plus a risk premium to assess whether or not to invest in assets considered riskier than bank deposits. This provides guidance for stock and real estate and other investment purchases. A similar approach can help you get started.

You start with the current interest rate paid on 90 Treasury Bills, or the current money market rate. In the storm build up, the Federal

Reserve has kept these rates artificially low under the guise of stimulating the economy.

In 2020 these rates were less than one percent. You can use whatever rates are current to set your asset allocation following the schedule below:

		Expected Return
Cash	2%	2.0%
Short Term Bonds	Cash plus 1%	3.0%
Medium Term Bonds	Cash plus 1.5%	3.5%
Stocks	Short term bonds plus 3%	6.0%
Real estate	Medium term bonds plus 2%	5.5%
Commodities	Short term bonds plus 4%	7.0%

Risk premiums, the percentage number additive noted above, vary with time. As with everything else in retirement these are subject to volatility. When the market is at new highs, these premiums are lower. Conversely, when the markets are at new lows, they are higher.

The above expected returns can help you set your beginning asset allocation. You need to invest your savings so the likelihood of what you earn will be greater than your Drawdown Ratio. In our ongoing example, the total expected return should be equal to or more than 3.8%.

In a very low interest rate environment this requires you to take on more investment risk than you might otherwise. When interest rates rise you can shift to higher interest paying investments and tamper down your risk.

The Longlifer 1, 2, 3 Retirement Portfolio serves as your guide to Purposeful Investing to help you through the coming years. In our example the $600,000 can be allocated as follows:

LONGLIFER 1.2.3
RETIREMENT PORTFOLIO

I	II		III		
A	A	B	A	B	C
$ 48,000	$24,000	$24,000	$204,000	$175,000	$125,000

In section I (A) you set aside your first year's income and one year's worth of savings as your safety fund, your 'rainy day' account. The purpose of this money is to allow you to head into the coming year knowing you have the income to meet your needs regardless of what the market does.

In our ongoing example, our couple would set aside nearly $24,000 to meet their first year income requirement. This money would be invested in principal protected short term CDs, Treasury Bills or money market funds. They would get a small amount of interest but have access to their cash, their principal protected and the knowledge they have the first year's income covered.

This fund would serve as the feeder fund to your bill paying account. To provide spending discipline, you would transfer $2,000 a month to your bill paying account. This would mimic your getting a paycheck. Spending more than $2,000 a month signals you to re-examine your spending plan or to identify underlying causes of excess spending.

If you are spending less than $2,000 a month, your bill paying account will accumulate a surplus. After a period of time, six months or so, you can re-examine your spending plan. If your spending will remain at this lower level, you can reduce your withdrawals and shift the surplus back into longer term investments.

The purpose of the second set aside would be to hold one year's worth of emergency funds equal to one year's income. This is to help you meet the unexpected. In this example, our couple would set aside an additional $24,000 into similar short- term principal protected investments.

While you worked, you may have used credit cards or a line of credit to meet unexpected expenses. This made sense in that you could keep your investment positions and use future money from your paychecks to repay the debt.

In retirement, there is no assurance of new money flowing in. What may start as a short- term debt may become permanent financing. You will find it hard to pay off this debt should your investments decline in value.

Although you would likely earn less on setting this money aside than long term investments, this account is part of your preparation to meet the unexpected. It offers you flexibility to anticipate and react to the storms' uncertainty.

In section II you set aside two additional years' worth of income. The purpose of this money is to add backup protection to help you survive long market declines. Money invested for higher returns generally require time and patience to reap the reward.

Two additional years of income provides reassurance that you will be alright and do not have to make hasty decisions in turbulent markets to make ends meet. Wealth quickly disappears when you sell losses and spend the proceeds.

The extra income protection allows you more choices on when and what to sell. It allows money to stay put and ride out market swings. Knowing your income is secure for three years gives you a different perspective on your other investments. There is less anxiousness and worry over the casino effect on daily valuations.

The second year and third year investments would be invested in short term bonds that mature in the second and third year. They provide a slightly higher interest rate than money market funds, but you are assured to get your principal back at maturity. If $24,000 is invested for each of these years, the interest credited can serve as an inflation offset.

In sections I and II you would set aside roughly 15-20% of your total savings. Its purpose is income security and predictability. The remaining money then can be invested with a longer-term perspective to meet other purposes of your savings plan.

The purpose of the money in Section III is long term financial security. This money moves from the safety of home and ventures out into the world. Measured risk is taken to gain the chance of earning higher returns.

You'll be living twenty to thirty years in retirement and most likely won't be able to get by on short-term interest rates. Health and other retirement costs will be shifted to you from the government. Inflation will erode your holdings and age will bring on a new set of costs.

To protect yourself you will need to need to have money designated to meet these challenges. Your principal will need to grow if it is to provide higher future income. You'll need to protect the purchasing power of your wealth from inflation and currency devaluation if you are to maintain your lifestyle throughout retirement.

The purpose of Section IIIA money is for guaranteed long term income and to offset longevity risk. This can be in the form of long- term bonds or similar contracts where you are able to hold your investments until maturity.

It could include insurance products like annuities. Annuities can provide additional income that you can't outlive. They are guaranteed contracts with insurance companies. IIIA allows for some of your money to be set aside for a longer period of time to provide you with higher income.

The purpose of Section IIIB money is to grow your principal. This is money that can be set aside for three years or more and can be invested in stocks and other assets whose primary characteristic is price appreciation.

The purpose of Section IIIC money is to protect your purchasing power. This money would be geared to take advantage of inflation and currency devaluation. Your funds could be invested in gold and precious metals or commodities like food and energy. As inflation increases these investments tend to rise in value.

Section III would have roughly 80 - 85% of our example portfolio. Our couple had a total of $600,000 so about $500,000 would be invested in Section III. Depending on your risk tolerance and how you see the near term, you would spread this money among the three silos.

As circumstance change and your perspective changes you would change the amounts in each silo. If you thought inflation is coming on strong, you could shift money from long term income to precious metals and commodities. If you soured on the stock market you could shift funds to the other silos.

With Sections I and II taking care of your daily spending needs, Section III money can focus on protecting your wealth in both real and inflationary terms. Although the money would be set aside for a longer period of time the storm's disruptions make this the part of your savings that requires active management.

With your initial positions set, you would make automatic adjustments at the beginning of each year. Accumulated long term interest in silo IIIA would shift to Section IIB to replace your third year income.

Section IIB would move up to IIA and become the second year's income. While IIA moves to replace the funds consumed in Section I. Each year there would be this waterfall effect continuously keeping three years income set aside in a protected state while the risk money can be targeted and managed to meet long term needs.

Purposeful Investing helps you meet the strategic objectives of your savings plan. You have reliable and sustainable income portioned out in three-year segments. The investment silos in Section III can help you protect and grow principal and combat potential inflation.

When you have three years income and a safety reserve, the pressure on the income source side of your Drawdown Ratio is effectively managed. If problems arise, they will first be noticed in the silos giving you a multi-year heads' up.

Now you can concentrate on the income need side of the Drawdown Ratio. If you are managing your money with your Expense Plan you should be able to better control your lifestyle elements. This leaves the unexpected and the potential expense shift to anticipate. To give you a leg up on this uncertainty you have set aside your safety reserve.

Tactical Portfolio Design

A study done in the late 1980's showed 94% of the return on your investments you received was due to your asset allocation. The remainder came from investment and security selection; that is selecting stocks, bonds and mutual funds.

This was touted by the financial advisory community of the importance of asset allocation which happens to be one of their competitive capabilities. Asset allocation lends itself to a form of sophisticated statistical analysis beyond the capabilities of regular investors. The statistical analysis of course, was based on historical returns and assumed everything was random.

Another misconception was the advisors assumed the 94% was from their value added. Usually, when this was explained to clients it showed the 94% on the upside. But, the study indicated your allocation was directly linked to both the upside and the downside.

A more subtle part of the study mostly glossed over by the advisors was 75% of the return came from you simply deciding to move your money from a cash account to an investment account. This is not necessarily attributed to the valued advice from your advisor but simply your own personal recognition to invest your savings.

Still the difference of 19% of your return to be explained by how you spread your money among stocks, bonds and other investments is something that you can use to your advantage. It requires you, or someone, to undertake some research and analysis to find the best way to spread your money around.

The asset allocation is part of both your risk management and your strategic portfolio design. Your strategic portfolio design sets the strategic allocation. It's now time to implement your strategy.

The remaining 6% also requires attention and is part of your tactical portfolio design. In our example the goals of the tactical design are:

- Decision making
- Selection process
- Flexibility

Decision Making

You may make the decisions on your own or you may seek advice. Nevertheless, you make the final decisions. You can't abdicate this responsibility. You need to decide if you will make all or some of the decisions.

Someone needs to determine the asset allocation, select specific investments, monitor results and make adjustments when necessary. You can choose from three basic models for effective decision making:

- Do it all yourself
- Hire a Captive Advisor
- Hire an Independent Advisor

Do It Yourself

The do-it-yourself model provides you with the most control and the lowest cost. It also places the responsibility of results squarely on your shoulders. If you are confident in your skills and research abilities, this can be the easiest and most private way to manage your savings.

The problems for most do-it-yourselfers are they tend to hold on to losses and fail to take gains. It seems to be a psychological thing. This can lead you to keep bad investments indefinitely and not repositioning this dead money and watching gains dissipate in the next market correction. Overtime, you could find yourself dead in the water.

If you invest on your own you need research and analytical capabilities. You need to set buy and sell criteria. You also need to have the capability to measure total performance to ensure you are beating your Drawdown Ratio. This requires time and attention that could compete with your leisure activities.

It would also be helpful for you to have a sounding board somewhere. Someone or some group where you can vet your ideas, get new insights and keep a heads up on what lies ahead. The storm will change investment interactions. Swift response requires knowing where you are at all times.

Captive Advisor

Captive advisors work for some umbrella organization. They will be agents or representatives of those entities. Usually, they are linked to insurance or security brokerage companies. These are the companies you are familiar with through various media advertising and their size and familiarity provide some comfort.

Captive advisors provide products, services and advice. They can do the buying, selling and reporting for you. They are paid by commissions or fees. It's important for you to know how your advisor gets paid in order to determine the value of their advice, any conflicts-of-interest and the quality of their products.

Advisors paid by commission are transaction oriented. They only can sell products approved by their companies for which they are licensed. This limits what they offer. These advisors are salespeople, not trusted advisors. They provide product information, say on an annuity or a mutual fund and can help you select a product from their mix.

Their advice is not objective. There is a tendency to guide you to the higher commission paying products and their loyalty is to the product supplier not you. They can be helpful if you need to buy something specific where you need product information and move on.

Regardless of what they may say, they do not monitor and manage the product once it's sold. Security regulations prevent them from recommending sell decisions on something they told you to buy and made a commission.

If you use a commission advisor much of the monitoring and ongoing changes to your savings will be up to you. These advisors simply help you buy something.

Advisors paid by fees tend to be more advice driven than product driven. They can take on more of the work to help you set your asset allocation. They can monitor and recommend changes to your savings plan. Since they are paid a fee on your overall savings, there is little incentive for them to buy and sell securities unnecessarily to generate commissions.

Their fee provides them less money up front but more over time if they are doing the job and you continue to retain them. There is a greater alignment of their interest with your interest. They know they can be fired and tend to be results driven.

However, their loyalty is ultimately to the organization; they don't have a fiduciary obligation to you to put your interest first. This leads to conflicts-of-interest with their service and advice to you.

Their organization requires them to meet revenue targets if they are to keep their job. This requirement tends to create substantial turnover and you may find yourself regularly working with a new advisor.

Their fee is layered on top of other fees paid to investment managers and could lead to total annual charges of over 2%. This can be a strong headwind to your results in a low return environment.

The captive advisor potentially can provide world class products under the umbrella of a large organization. The large organization provides deep pockets if things go wrong. They can serve as a one-stop shop for your financial needs.

However, they can't report on what they don't hold. If you have holdings with other companies you would still need to conduct total performance analysis to see if you are beating your Drawdown Ratio.

They also rarely recommend selling current positions. This resulted in huge losses to clients during the 2008 market meltdown. You would need to initiate discussions on whether to hold or sell underperforming or high risk positions.

Independent Advisor

Independent advisors are Registered Investment Advisors, (RIA) and are regulated by the state or the Securities Exchange Commission (SEC). They have a legal fiduciary responsibility to place your interest before their interest and tend to provide the most objective and conflict-free advice.

They are smaller firms than the captive companies and have less capital to maintain technology and cover things should something go awry. But most of them partner with larger independent companies to provide critical functions like custody of assets and trading platforms. This partnering provides you with an additional layer of regulatory protection.

RIAs are fee based advisors; they are not allowed to accept commissions or other compensation separate from their fee. This tends to align their interest with yours. They tend to be investment managers or portfolio managers. Each model has advantages and disadvantages.

Investment managers buy and sell securities on your behalf. They tend to have high minimum investment hurdles usually $100,000 or more. They will report performance and manage part or all of your savings. There is a high degree of transparency and generally you know what you are getting.

But, investment managers can't be expert in all areas of investing. This leads them to specialize in stocks or bonds. Working with investment managers limits your asset allocation options as you only can invest in what they offer.

These managers generally don't provide strategic asset allocation advice and won't report on your investments not held with them. Since they are quite busy tending to daily investment management, they rarely offer other financial or retirement planning advice. However, they tend to provide low-cost investment management and high levels of client service.

There are two broad types of portfolio managers. They provide either a closed model or an open model choice of investments. The closed model has the advisor managing managers.

The closed model advisors provide asset allocation advice and implement their advice through other managers. These managers may be mutual funds, separate accounts or other pooled investment products. Their investment options are limited to the managers at hand. This could limit the type of assets in which you could invest.

They report on only what they oversee. If you have IRAs, 401(k) s, bank deposits not held by them, you would still need to conduct your own comprehensive review of your investments. Also. these advisors tend to focus on investing and usually don't provide comprehensive financial or retirement planning.

As an overseer, there is an additional layer of costs. You pay for the asset allocation and the individual investment manager. Total cost usually is between 1 -2% per year. You can have them manage all of your money, with noted limitations, or you could simply give them part of your overall savings.

The open model advisors provide the greatest breadth of investment options. Essentially, you could invest in nearly anything, including private holdings. In the open model the advisor focuses on both the strategic and tactical asset allocation and investment selection.

They can bring in outside managers, mutual funds, ETFs commodities and so on to provide a fully diversified portfolio. This model also can allow you to add your particular investment picks to the mix and get a comprehensive report on your holdings.

They tend to be more of a personal advisor than an investment manager. Many have the capability to help you with other financial and retirement planning concerns. They can hire and fire managers on your behalf and switch holdings quickly and easily. They usually charge .5%-1% per year.

There are separate charges for outside managers, transactions costs and costs particular to specific investments. Generally, your overall cost should be under 2% per year. You tend to get personalized service and objective advice.

You can choose to invest on your own or work with an advisor. Either way, someone must determine your asset allocation, specific investments and comprehensive reporting and analysis. You are the decision maker and need to be involved in how your money is managed. The storm will punish those who invest and forget.

Selection Process

Your asset allocation targets specific dollar amounts toward each section of your investment plan. Whether you work alone or with an advisor, the next step is to invest the targeted money into specific securities. Even if you work with an advisor it's still important you have a basic understanding of what's going on. As a better informed consumer, you can better protect your nest egg.

In section I(A) you'll set aside one year's income for spending and an additional year's income for your rainy-day account. In our example, this amounts to two separate investments of $24,000.

The $24,000 for income should be invested in securities that won't lose principal value. They should pay a competitive interest and give you easy access to your cash. There should be no or very little charge to holding these investments.

Appropriate investments would include money market accounts, bank and credit union accounts, short term savings accounts, 90 treasury bills and interest-bearing checking accounts. The money held in these investment accounts should be capable of being easily transferred to your bill paying account.

The money set aside in your rainy-day account should also have principal protection. The purpose of this money is to be available when you are hit with an unexpected expense. You don't want to have to take investment losses or taxable gains to meet an unexpected expense.

You need quick access to the money and it should be kept separate from your spending account to ensure it is kept for its purpose. This money could be invested in rolling 90 Treasury Bills, which can be bought without charge from the Federal Reserve.

You could also invest in one-year CDs, global CDs, those denominated in a foreign currency like Swiss Francs or Australian Dollars. These could provide a bit more interest but still keep your principal safe.

Section II(A) can be invested in securities with a two- year maturity. This $24,000 is set aside to provide your income in year two. Extending the maturity of your investments provides a higher interest rate that can build up until its needed in year two.

Typical investments could be government bonds maturing in one year, one-year CDs domestic or foreign. If you are in a high tax bracket short term Municipal bonds could provide tax free interest. These investments could lose principal if you sell them before their maturity date. But given the purpose of this money and the rest of your allocation, this is unlikely.

Section II(B) is similar to (A) except your target date is two years. This allows for the $24,000 plus interest to be shifted to the short- term investments in Section I(A) in the beginning of year three.

Section III is a bit more complicated and forms your longer-term investment strategy. The new retiree will need to secure long-term income, principal growth and inflation protection. Each purpose has a different set of investments to accomplish these objectives.

Silo *III (A)* seeks long term income. Money invested for longer periods of time tends to require higher interest payments. Over time, declining credit quality and rising interest rates are two critical risks you'll face and you need additional compensation to cover these risks.

Governments around the world are adding debt as never before in history. The mountain of debt taken on by various European countries is now affecting their credit ratings. The credit rating of the US now gets periodic review by the ratings agencies. In the past, the review was cursory, now its attentive.

Rising interest rates are the biggest bane to bonds and other income securities. When interest rates rise, bond values fall; it's simple math. For example, let's say you have a $10,000 bond paying two percent interest per year. Each year you get $200.

Fast forward, and interest rates rise to four percent. Who would buy your bond at the lower interest rate when they could get a new bond at a higher interest rate? If you had to sell your bond you would have to make it equivalent to the new four percent interest rate.

How do you do this? You would have to lower the price of your bond to $5,000. At this price, the $200 annual interest rate equals four percent and your bond is now competitive in the market. As you can see, there is the risk of substantial losses in bonds when interest rates are rising.

Currently, we are in the lowest interest rate environment since World War II. The Federal Reserve is flooding the economy with cash. Any up tick in the economy or hints of inflation will send interest rates rising and bond prices falling.

The money you allocated to long term income could sit temporarily in a money market account until interest rates rise and find a new level of stability. At that time, you could place your investments.

Interest rates have been low for some time and some economists fear short term deflation, which would be good for bonds. As usual the markets remain uncertain. But, should you decide to invest there are ways you can mitigate the risks.

One way to avoid principal loss is to not have to sell the bonds or income securities before maturity. If you hold the bond until maturity you get your money back. If interest rise during the holding period, you are just out not earning a higher rate. One way to ensure you get your principal back and participate in changing interest rates is to ladder your investments.

Laddering, simply is buying individual bonds with different maturity rates. In our example, we have $200,000 targeted to long term income. This money could be equally split into four purchases of bonds where they mature in 3, 4, 5, and 6 years.

You would get higher interest rates than short term investments and if you hold the bonds until maturity you get your money back. But, if interest rates rise, you have part of your money maturing in three years that could be invested at the new higher rates. Each subsequent year you get proceeds from a maturing bond that could be reinvested at the new rates.

Another way to lessen the risk of holding bonds is to buy TIPS and WIPS. These are inflation protected government bonds. TIPS are Treasury inflation protected securities and WIPS are world inflation protected securities.

If inflation increases and interest rates rise, these securities adjust the interest paid to reflect the higher inflation. This increase in interest paid helps to protect your principal. In the times ahead the best bond alternative would be to buy laddered TIPS and WIPS. Although, they still could lose value if interest rates rise to an expanding economy and inflation remains flat.

Instead of buying bonds as individual securities you also can buy them in investment packages like mutual funds and ETFs (electronically traded funds). The packages offer professional management for a fee. In a low return environment this .5-1% annual fee may eat up most of your gains.

Another drawback is mutual funds and ETF have no maturity date. You can't hold them until they mature like individual bonds and get your entire principal back. These funds trade bonds. The trading can increase your payments at the expense of a lower account value. You can lose a lot of money with bond funds in an increasing interest rate environment.

Some of the money in this section could be used to offset longevity risk. There is a concern that new retirees have about outliving their money. You could supplement your Social Security with a guaranteed monthly income stream from an immediate annuity.

Immediate annuities are contracts with insurance companies to provide a fixed monthly income for the rest of your life, no matter how long you live in exchange for a up front lump sum deposit. The insurance company takes the risk of you living beyond life expectancy and pools your money with other investors.

Your payments consist of interest and principal and consequently are higher than if you only took out interest from an investment. Here, you are consuming principal. These payments are fixed and their value is eroded by inflation over time. You also give up access to this cash as you are only entitled to the monthly payment.

Still, in Purposeful Investing, annuities can make sense. You may want to link a fixed income amount with a fixed expense amount. You might decide to cover your mortgage, property taxes and a stipend amount for food and medicine with fixed sources of income.

Let's say these expenses are $2,000 per month. If your Social Security and pension total $1,300 you might get an immediate annuity to make up the $700 a month difference. This can provide peace of mind in the case the investment world falls apart; you still have income to cover your basic living needs.

The balance of your investments can be considered variable income. That is, when there is extra income beyond your basic needs you can splurge and when there isn't you can tighten. Annuities are valued at current interest rates and it may make sense to wait until rates rise before committing.

Silo *III (B)* uses a portion of your investment portfolio to grow principal. Investments in this section will be mostly stocks. When the economy recovers business increases and the value of stocks should increase.

But as you have seen in the last decade increases can be ephemeral. To realize gains from your stock investments you need to have a buy and sell strategy and select stocks that pay dividends.

If your stock goes up and you sell it you get real gains. Similarly, if the stock pays dividends you get real money. It's not just a price appreciation game as appreciation can easily be corrected by depreciation.

In our example, $100,000 would be invested in global large companies like Coca Cola, Johnson and Johnson, Toyota and so forth. These companies pay dividends and get their revenues worldwide thus providing some protection for a falling dollar.

Being global and large demonstrates they have a working business model and one that should weather the storm. The companies you select should also have pricing power where they can pass on inflation through higher prices. These companies should do well in an inflationary environment.

To add a turbo charge to the portfolio $45,000 should be invested in emerging markets like China, Korea and India. These countries will grow substantially faster than the US. Although these markets are volatile, investments here should add growth to your portfolio.

The remaining $30,000 should be invested in small and mid size US companies. These are companies that keep the everyday activity going in the country. Smaller companies are tend to be more volatile and risky. Having your first three years income covered you should be able to ride the valuation waves and add growth to your investments.

You can buy these securities individually or through managed and unmanaged packages like mutual funds and ETFs. You can make all of the decisions yourself or work with an advisor in the selection process.

If you decide to purchase individual securities yourself you should be skilled in security valuation. If you lack this skill don't buy individual securities. Buy them in their packaged form.

Separate account managers, mutual funds, variable annuities and ETFs are the most prevalent forms of investment packages. As with most things, each has its advantages and disadvantages.

Separate accounts managers buy and sell securities for your private account. Your money is not pooled with other investors. This results in lower administration costs and usually greater tax efficiency than mutual funds.

They usually have high minimum investment amounts beginning at $100,000. Fees generally start at 1% and decline as your balance increases. Each manager tends to specialize resulting in your need to have multiple managers to manage a diversified portfolio.

This requires you to set aside a substantial amount of money to be available for stocks. Annual costs tend to be lower than mutual funds and you have some flexibility in what is purchased. For example, if you don't want tobacco stocks and such things.

Objective performance information is not as available as it is for mutual funds making the selection process more difficult. To get this information you would need to go through an investment advisor.

It's also important to remember that you hired these managers to buy stocks. This means no matter how lousy the market is they will buy stocks. They also will not fire themselves. If the markets are lousy, they aren't going to tell you to withdraw your money. You need to do this yourself.

Mutual funds are a version of separate account management for the masses. There are over 4,000 funds. Your money is pooled with other investors allowing you to get greater diversification. This larger amount of pooled money then can be managed by a professional money manager.

Costs are higher; generally, .8 to 2.5% per year. Their management fees do not decline with an increasing balance. Cash needs to be set aside for redemptions so you are never fully invested.

Mutual funds hold income tax surprises. They are flow-through entities for tax purposes. This means they don't pay taxes you as the account holder do. Interest, dividends and capital gains, not capital losses, are passed on to you whether you receive the distribution or not.

When you buy a mutual fund, it has an existing income tax liability in accumulated dividends and gains that have not been sold. As long as you hold your position you potentially can get hit with a tax bill.

The funds distribute the gains, usually near the end of the year. Buying funds at this time can lead you into a tax trap. Taxes are paid buy the account holder on the distribution date regardless of how long you have held the fund.

For example, if you put $10,000 into a fund on October 31, and the fund made a 10% distribution on November 1, you would have to pay taxes on $1,000. In a sense your principal is returned to you as a taxable gain. Do not do this.

The effectiveness of mutual fund managers is hard to evaluate. There are all sorts of companies doing evaluations assigning stars, points and grades. But, all of this is based on hindsight and historical analysis. They do a good job of explaining what happened.

Unfortunately, all of this analysis is not very good a predicting how the funds will perform going forward. Most of the analysis is a waste of time. Studies consistently show top managers during one five-year period severely under perform in the subsequent five-year period.

Similarly, funds that did great last year tend to do poorly the following year. Much of this is due to luck. One theme may be hot one year, like tech stocks, and the next year nobody wants them. Buying on recent past performance tends to have you buying at the top.

Average performance is misleading as most averages are. Many times, the average is influenced by one out of the ordinary year. Using the analysis does not warn you of a coming bad year or the likelihood of getting an exceptional year.

For most managers you can't distinguish between luck and skill. Most don't beat an unmanaged index benchmark. If their management can't beat an unmanaged index, why pay them?

Where you can use the analysis of those rating agencies is to focus on fees and whether the manager beats the index. If fees are low and performance is above the benchmark this could be a good fund. You should also look at the worst performing year to see if you have the tolerance to suffer such losses.

If you feel mutual fund managers aren't worth the cost you can invest in indexed mutual funds and ETFs. Index funds hold a variety of stocks in some predetermined proportion. They don't buy and sell to get performance.

They just represent some segment of the market and your risk and return reflect that segment. Their costs are much lower, generally .25-.75%. They don't need all of the research and investment staff managed funds need.

ETFs are like index funds but have a different legal structure. These funds buy and sell like stocks. There is less administration and generally cost less than index funds. You can buy and sell positions throughout the day where index funds only allow end of day trades.

ETFs add more flexibility at a lower cost to your portfolio. They have become quite popular with the professional investor over the last couple of years. You can get diversification and target specific segments of the investment world for a low cost.

Silo *III C* money provides inflation protection. Your first brush with inflation will come from the prices you pay for things. Health insurance premiums and out-of-pocket health costs will surely rise. You'll notice grocery and restaurant prices going up along with entertainment expenses and energy.

You'll be able to measure the impact on your cost of living through your Expense and Activity Plan. This offers you some opportunity to change the way you spend money to counteract the rising costs.

Inflation lowers the purchasing power of your savings if you don't take appropriate action. Rising prices and falling purchasing power will stretch you like a rubber band. As stress build up something has to give.

To relieve the stress of declining savings purchasing power you can invest in those items that tend to go up in price. This tends to be first noticed in raw materials, food and energy. These price increases are passed on to you quickly in the form of higher grocery and gasoline prices. Your retirement activities may not change but the cost of doing them will increase.

There are two long term trends that will keep pressure on rising prices. First, millions of people in the developing world, notably China, India and Brazil, will move from poverty to relative middle class. Most will seek to live the western lifestyle of better food and higher energy consumption.

Second, is government policy. The massive debt of government will lower the value of paper currency. Compounding this devaluation will be inflationary policies of flooding economies with cash. All of this money needs to go somewhere. If businesses don't invest in new projects this money will head toward prices.

During the years of the storm, all of this will need to be sorted out. In the meantime you need to have a portion of your savings geared towards inflation protection. Instead of thinking of investing in cars, hamburgers and handbags, think corn, oil and copper. A portion of your savings needs to be invested in real assets.

You can protect against purchasing power loss by investing in raw materials, food, and energy. This can be done by investing in companies and investment products that manage these commodities. This lets you take advantage of the increasing worldwide demand for basic living materials.

Another component of your inflation silo should be precious metals. Metals like gold, silver and platinum tend to serve as stores of value when currencies are being debased. As the storm re-sorts government policies its unclear which countries will follow fiscal responsibility and which will let things ride. The price of gold tends to be the scorekeeper.

You can buy into this asset class in four different ways:
1. Stocks
2. Trusts and Partnerships
3. Direct Participation
4. Options

You can buy stocks in companies whose main line of business is commodity related. For example, you could buy large oil companies and wholesale food companies. These companies have commodity assets on their balance sheet and if market prices for those commodities rise and are expected to hold that increase, the value of the companies should rise.

You still have stock market risk but value could be better maintained in an inflationary environment. These companies could also be bought through specialized mutual fund and ETF packages.

The trust form of ownership requires that at least 95 percent of earning flow to the trust holders. This makes this a high yield type of investment. The most popular forms of trust ownership are Canadian Trusts and Real Estate Trusts (REITS).

Canadian Trusts primarily hold natural resources like timber, copper, gold and energy. These are operating business and therefore have management risk. Most of them trade on the exchanges and carry trading risk. Their market price can go up or down. This volatility is tempered by the high yield 6-7 percent range in this low interest environment and provides some downside protection.

REITS can get you into the commercial real estate market. Here, value is determined by leases. These are contracts that provide steady income and usually contain annual inflation increases. These market REITS have trading risk and management risk but can provide a steadily increasing yield.

Partnerships, mostly Master Limited Partnerships, (MLP) are legal structures mostly holding energy related assets like pipelines and natural gas storage. These are operating business and carry management risk.

The businesses produce steady and predictable revenue as energy still needs to move through the country regardless of the inflationary environment. The partnerships are required to pay out nearly all of their earned income resulting in a high yield investment also in the 7 percent range.

The dividends are partially sheltered by business deductions allowing you to hold on to more of the distribution. They do have partnership tax complexities if you hold them directly and you should review these prior to making an investment. You can avoid the tax complexities by buying MLPs through specialized mutual fund and ETF packages.

Direct participation gives you an ownership interest in an active business. This is usually in the form of a Limited Partnership (LP) holding. The LP limits your liability at the expense of control. Typical programs include equipment leasing, oil and gas and real estate and entice you by high yields.

General partners have control and can do pretty much whatever they want. These deals are high cost, 15-25% up front costs, and are loaded with conflicts-of-interest. Most of these deals do not serve the investor well.

There is a lot of dishonesty, fraud and abuse in these programs. To find a good program read the cost and conflicts-of-interest section of the prospectus carefully. Choose only programs that have run a complete cycle, have paid back their investors and have low up-front costs.

These programs require a long-term commitment; mostly 5 -10 years. This locks up your money and there is little you can do if the program fails to meet its objectives.

Options let you take advantage of short-term changes in commodity prices usually through the form of futures contracts. These contracts lock in prices for 30-90 days although some last considerably longer.

If you think prices will be different at the end of the contract than what the market is betting on today, you can make money. If inflation rises faster than expected, these contract values will increase and you can use inflation to your advantage. But if you know little or nothing about options don't buy them.

If you still would like access to the asset class, you can invest in Managed Futures programs. Professionals, for a fee, buy and sell options according to their trading philosophy. There are good programs and bad programs. You generally would have to buy these through a brokerage firm or financial advisor.

The good ones will have a relatively stable rate of return in the 6-9% range. They use options to both manage risk of market declines and to take advantage of rising markets. These programs can be used to provide downside protection to your overall investment portfolio.

You can buy and own commodities directly. Gold and silver coins tend to be the most widely held. There are high commissions on buying and selling these coins and you may be better served owning gold through an ETF.

Flexibility

One ongoing storm survival tactic is to anticipate and react quickly to change. To do this you need to structure flexibility into your current position while keeping an eye on the horizon. If you see things happening but can't react because your current position has you stuck in the mud, the damage from the storm can be severe.

When investing you need to commit to a longer time period to get higher rates of return. But while waiting this longer period, you cannot be sure if you will ride out the storm or crash ashore. To maneuver through the storm, you need to be at the helm.

As you likely experienced in the last decade, a buy-and-hold strategy can be costly. You need to get information, process it and make changes in a timely manner if you are to manage and grow your wealth over the coming decades.

Flexibility can be built into your plan by limiting the amount of your savings tied up in investments you can't access and by having the ability to quickly sell investments to minimize or avoid losses.

Some investments require you to tie up your money for a long period of time if you are to get the higher return. This can by long term CDs, bonds you will hold until maturity, annuities with surrender charges and partnerships with withdrawal restrictions.

Giving up access to your cash to get a higher return isn't necessarily bad. It makes sense for bonds you will hold to maturity and can make sense for the other noted investments. The thing to keep in mind, is not to have too much of your money tied up in illiquid investments. The maximum you should allocate to these types of investments is 20%.

Additional flexibility is built in through the process of investing. Each year you will begin your plan with the outlook you have for the coming year. This will guide your decisions on how you will spread your money across the silos, or the different purposes you have identified in the coming year.

This defines your investment mindset for the year. Your investments should begin on the first floor of the investment building, that is, fundamentals. You make adjustments by the second-floor trends. Throughout the year you monitor the trends and if they change you change your investments.

You need to review your investments at least quarterly. You should ask yourself if things have changed since you made your initial investment choices. If your mindset or outlook has changed, you should change your positions. If things haven't changed and your investments are on track, you're set until the next quarterly review.

Knowing you can change investments along with a process to rationally review them for potential change, offers you the maximum flexibility to manage your way through the storm.

You have now completed the first four steps. You have a snapshot of where you are today and where you want to go tomorrow. Now it's time to put things into motion.

Chapter 10

EVALUATION – STEP 5

Just because you intend something doesn't make it so. Just because you plan something doesn't make it happen. Your fortuitous march through the Stages of Retirement brings good things and bad things. It takes effort to ensure the good things outweigh the bad things.

Most people view tomorrow as an incremental change from today. It's hard to make sense of things years ahead. This incremental view may help them deal with the unknown affect of the accumulated tomorrows. They figure if they deal with today tomorrow will take care of itself.

That works for some things. Not for others. It's the others that require your attention. Those other things out there will make one of your tomorrows quite different than today. Your plan is an effort to identify and prepare for those other things.

This effort may seem a waste of effort but to move forward it helps to know where you are going. Aimlessness does give you flexibility since you can go anywhere and claim where you end up a success. Though, this ping-pong approach to your retirement results in ever increasing vulnerability and insecurity.

Most assuredly what actually happens to you will differ from your plan. Yet planning is important. It provides reference points. It gives you the stars to navigate your way through the ocean of retirement.

To move intelligently through uncharted territory, you need to know where you are and where you want to go. This establishes your starting and ending points. The multitude of choices and options narrows. Your attention focuses on the trajectory.

You defined your starting point in steps 1-4. These steps define where you are today. You know basically how much money you need and how much money you have saved. This serves as your mooring post, a familiar and safe place. Step 5, takes where you are today and projects where you want to go. It provides the ending point to help you set your retirement direction.

This requires you to learn or enhance three basic skills:
- Projection
- Measurement
- Evaluation

Your plan projections begin with your imagination. You need to step outside your today self and imagine what tomorrow will be like. You can use likely events, goals, and objectives to shape how you want your future to look.

Many people monitor and budget their expenses. Some also evaluate their investment performance. This is important. Nevertheless, this is hindsight planning. You can learn a good deal of how you spend and invest money and this may change how you go about your daily life.

Yet to survive the storm you need to refine and enhance your efforts to take this hindsight and project what is likely to occur in the future to both your expenses and your savings. You may need to help your ill parents or move closer to your kids. You may have lost money in the market. Each of these affects your future lifestyle which in turn affects the amount of money you will need and the amount of money you have available.

To get a sense of how your lifestyle may change requires you to be the look-out for your plan. Hurricanes, tornadoes and blizzards provide some warning. This gives you time to make some preparations. Earthquakes, unpredictable in their timing and magnitude, require a different type of preparation.

History can provide guidance. Last years' budget and investment performance can provide you with some insight but it fails to give you a heads-up when you are about to step into something you would prefer to avoid. Projection provides the end point.

Next you connect the dots. There are many ways to get from your starting point to your ending point. It's not always a straight line. You can choose different trajectories. It's not so important whether these projections are right or wrong, they just need to be reasonable. This way they serve as shots in the dark lighting an area through which you can proceed.

To see if you are on track, you need to measure where you are and compare it to where you have been and where you want to go. Measurement provides orientation and keeps you from getting lost, losing control and being subject to the whims of uncertainty.

Measurement invariably leads to math. For some, your eyes may glaze over when tables of numbers are provided and someone who can work the numbers. For others, numbers are the raw meat potentially leading to a feeding frenzy of analysis and should seek occasional time outs to gain perspective.

You need to measure how much you are spending and compare it to what you planned on spending; what you earned on your investments with what you planned and track your drawdown ratio and other warning signals. You'll also need to assess whether you are meeting your personal and social goals.

Step 5, Evaluation, helps you determine if your projections are reasonable. It lets you know if retirement is feasible. If your retirement is feasible, evaluation helps you assess whether it is sustainable.

Evaluation interprets measurement results. These results will be both historical, what has happened, and projected, what is expected to happen. Either way, it's important to remember your projections are guesses. Just because they come out of a computer and are presented in four color presentations doesn't make them any more than guesses. They are as likely to be right as wrong. The test again is reasonableness.

Reasonableness begins with the assumptions you use. All of the analysis at the back end can appear silly if you start with silly assumptions. For example, you can assume 15% investment returns and zero inflation and suddenly your retirement looks bright.

These numbers may be at the extreme, but as you narrow them what estimates are likely? Being off one percent over 20-30 years can be the difference from living comfortably and moving in with the kids.

Evaluation makes sense of your projections and measurements. Projection takes the time to look about and target a spot on the horizon to guide you forward. Measurement assesses your daily slog through the pathways towards the horizon. Evaluation signals safety or danger and gives you options should change be required.

The pathways aren't always straight and true. Unexpected obstacles and washouts will block your path. As you move over or around them it's easy to lose your sense of direction. Projection gives you perspective, measurement gives you cause for action. Evaluation gives you intelligence.

Measurement gives your projections meaning. To navigate the storm you need to periodically measure what is actually happening with what you expected to happen. This ongoing evaluation helps you to make adjustments and recalibrate your trajectory.

Projection

Retirement Viability – Retirement Quick Test

It's hard to give much credibility to any projection thirty years into the future. This makes it impossible to ever truthfully answer the question of whether or not you will outlive your money. Instead, projections provide guidance to help you direct your day-to-day activities to reduce the chance of you running out of money.

The Quick Test lets you know if you are in the retirement ballpark or at least retirement city. Your projections help define the ballpark's location and dimensions. You should get some comfort if you find you're in the ballpark; it's a start. If you're not in the ballpark you've got work to do.

Reasonable projections follow reasonable assumptions. To determine your retirement viability, you need to make three critical assumptions.

1. Lifestyle
2. Inflation
3. Investment Return

Your lifestyle assumptions define your starting point; you're baseline. They create the structure and dimensions of your retirement. What you do and how you do it establishes your lifestyle spending patterns.

Your spending will change over time due to inflation and changes to your activities. Estimating your future costs let's you know how much income you'll need to maintain your lifestyle.

Your inflation assumptions set the trajectory of your expenses. This is the slope of your lifestyle needs. They provide the location coordinates of your retirement ballpark. Higher inflation assumptions push the ballpark away from you. Lower assumptions keep it local.

The returns you think you can get from your savings sets the parameters of your retirement. They give the ballpark dimension. Higher investment return assumptions enlarge the ballpark making it easier to hit. Lower investment returns give you a little league park.

For example, we will use our imaginary couple to set the lifestyle assumptions. Further we'll assume the current Federal Reserve inflation target of 2% and the 6% investment return our couple assumed they could achieve when they calculated their drawdown ratio.

Our couple needs roughly $24,000 today to maintain their lifestyle. They have saved roughly $600,000. Both of these numbers will fluctuate over time. To freeze-frame it we will apply the straight line assumptions above to see how they are doing 20 years from now.

You can multiply the 2% annual increase to the spending twenty times or use a Future Value Factor (FVF) to simply the calculations. The FVF simply adds one and raises the calculation to the twentieth power. It looks like this: $(1.02)^{20}$. The .02 is the 2% inflation rate expressed in decimal form. The FVF becomes 1.486.

Twenty years from now what our couple is spending today will require they spend $35,664 to simply maintain their lifestyle.

What happens to their investments is a bit more complicated. It requires two steps. Although they assume they will earn 6%, remember they are taking money out each year so what's left to grow their principal is less than 6%. First, they need to subtract their Drawdown Ratio from their investment return. Their ratio was 3.8%. This leaves their principal growth rate to be 2.2% or 6%-3.8%.

Using the same FVF formula $(1.022)^{20}$ the investment FVF is 1.545. This is multiplied times their $600,000 to get an expected value twenty years from now of $927,000.

At first blush you'll notice their investment principal grows faster than their expenses. If they are fine today, they should be fine with this set of simple assumptions. This is one reason not to deceive yourself with overly optimistic investment returns because they will show you are better off than you likely will be.

The couple's new Drawdown Ratio, money needed from investments divided by total investments, $35,664/$927,000 remains 3.8%. There is a slight decrease but its several decimal places back.

Under this set of assumptions, the Retirement Quick Test shows the couple to have a sustainable retirement. Also, notice that they are twenty years older and can tolerate a higher Drawdown Ratio subsequently by maintaining things they are in a more secure position.

You can use the FVF formula to make approximations of where you are today and check how your Drawdown Ratio changes. You also can use your desired Drawdown Ratio to target a savings amount you'll need if your retirement is years off.

You start by determining how much income you need from your investments. This is your total living expense less Social Security, pensions and other contractual income. Next you divide this number by your Drawdown Ratio to get your savings target.

For example, let's say you need $3,000 a month or $36,000 per year, from your savings and you wish to limit your Drawdown Ratio to 4%. Simply divide your annual spending by your Drawdown Ratio – 36,000/.04 = $900,000. If you choose a riskier retirement with a Drawdown Ratio of 5% your savings target shrinks to $720,000.

As you can see the numbers are fluid and security relative. The Retirement Quick Test is a ballpark estimate. When you get closer or more serious about retiring, you'll need to refine this approach.

Retirement Viability - Refined Test

The Retirement Quick Test makes some unrealistic assumptions. It doesn't take into account likely lifestyle changes during your stay in retirement. It assumes all of your expenses will increase by the same inflation rate. It also assumes constant investment returns and income taxes.

You begin to refine your projections with better lifestyle assumptions. The amount of something you consume or your activity level and price changes or inflation ultimately drives your lifestyle cost.

Your consumption patterns and the things you do will change during retirement. When you capture the most obvious changes you refine your projections. For example, you may travel a lot in the early years of retirement and less so later. It doesn't make sense to take today's travel expenses and assume they will continue throughout retirement.

There may be family changes like caring your aging parents. You may actively participate in a hobby today that seems less interesting to pursue twenty years from now. Your social and entertainment activities at some point will curtail.

Similarly, as you age, you likely will need additional personal services to assist you with health concerns and certain physical activities. Medicare kicks in at age 65. If you retire prior to 65 your health expenses are likely to drop once you qualify for Medicare.

Your activity and consumption level drive one point of your lifestyle expense. Inflation drives the other. Headline inflation, or the government proclamation of inflation is notoriously understated. This works to the government's advantage.

Tax brackets are indexed to inflation. If inflation is understated these brackets adjust less increasing tax revenue. It also slows inflation indexed payments for Social Security and other government programs.

Headline inflation does not work to your advantage. It tends to lull you into overlooking the steady creep of your cost-of-living. The cost of some things goes up faster than other things. Health cares expenses being one of those.

To make better projections you need to calculate your Personal Inflation Rate. Your PIR takes into consideration where you live. Large cities and certain states have higher inflation rates than others. It considers your basic lifestyle and how you choose to spend money to meet your retirement goals.

We are likely headed into an inflationary period of time. A simple one or two percent change each year becomes a lot of money when you project what it will cost you to live twenty years hence. The two percent headline inflation appears comforting but if you are spending most of your money on food, energy and health your PIR is likely double.

Categorizing your expenses help you make more realistic assumptions which in turn make your projections more realistic. You categorized your expenses in your Expense and Activity Plan. Those same categories can guide you to towards calculating a better projection of your lifestyle costs.

You can adjust each category by likely changes in your activity level and by your PIR to get a more realistic picture of what retirement will cost. Yet it's still hard to imagine how things will play out over the next 20-30 years.

One way to attack this task is to break it into smaller bite size pieces. You can use the Stages of Retirement to make your best guesses over five-year increments. This still doesn't guarantee the projections will match reality as you are trying to predict the future. But it does provide greater confidence in assessing your level of security in retirement.

Anticipation

If you are five or more years from retirement, the Quick Test may be all of the refinement you need. It provides you with a target savings goal and you have time to build savings and get better control over your lifestyle expenses.

Once you are in the five-year retirement zone, you need to pay more attention to detail. During this period, you should save as much as you can, pay off all consumer debt and lay the foundation for how your retirement will play out.

Your thinking needs to shift from what you are getting paid to what it costs you to live. You will need to subtract expenses you no longer will have to make once you retire and add the new retirement expenses to get your new lifestyle cost.

For example, let's say you make $100,000 a year. You don't take home $100,000 a year. Expenses like Social Security, Medicare and other payroll taxes will no longer be paid. However, you will still pay income taxes.

Deductions for employee benefits, pension contributions and like deductions go away. You won't be spending as much on clothes, dry cleaning, tools and ongoing education. Nor will you be spending as much on commute, parking and tolls.

By subtracting these expenses from your current income gets you a new baseline for what it will cost you to live. To this you add the new expenses to plan to make once you retire. This could include travel, hobbies additional forms of entertainment.

You may have to pay higher health insurance premiums from when you were employed. Dental, vision and prescription drug costs could also be higher if your employer covered these expenses. You now will have to pay estimated income taxes. Although this may not be an increased expense, the timing of payments changes as you no longer have payroll withholdings.

These adjustments give you your starting point to make your retirement projections. In our ongoing example, the starting point for our imaginary couple was their Expense and Activity Plan as follows.

		Personal
Personal Activities	$ 750	
Others' Activities	600	Daily walk
Home	2,000	Golf weekly
Health	500	Tennis twice weekly
Consumer Debt	200	Religious practice
General Living	1,000	Learn Mandarin
Total	$5,050	Backgammon
		Study astronomy
Income taxes @15%	$ 891	Creative activities
		Gardening
Total Monthly Expense	$5,941	Mediterranean Diet

DRAWDOWN SAFE ZONE
6% Investment Return

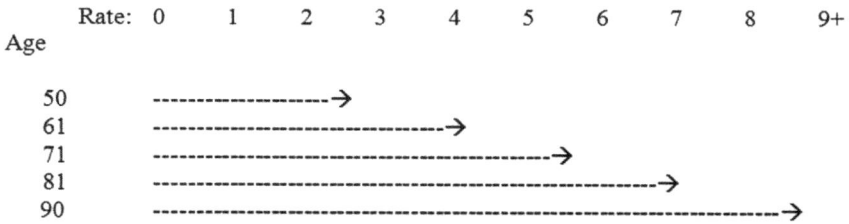

Age	Rate: 0	1	2	3	4	5	6	7	8	9+
50	--------------------→									
61	--------------------------------→									
71	--→									
81	--→									
90	--→									

Chapter 11

UNCERTAINTY

One thing that disrupts the best laid plans is the unexpected. By its nature it tends to show up when it is least expected and usually brings a magnitude of impact beyond your expectations.

Although you may have your lifestyle expenses and activities laid out, you still face the challenge of the unexpected. You may not have changed a thing in your life nor done nothing in particular to attract the unexpected yet it still can happen.

One ongoing challenge you will have throughout retirement is to figure whether or not you should prepare for the unexpected. Preparation usually requires money and time. You may choose not to spend money or time today to reduce a potential risk that may or may not happen tomorrow. But, should you choose to remain unprepared, you need to recognize you are taking the chance that something untoward may happen.

Some things are more likely than others. For example, the chances you will need to pay substantial medical costs are greater than the chance you will win the lottery. Here it makes more sense to prepare for potential medical expenses than is does for potential winnings.

To survive the approaching storm, you will need to decide how best to use your limited resources. If you spend money to reduce risk you have less money to produce income. Some risks you may want to insure while others you may take your chances. Either way, you need to make a clear-headed assessment of what is unexpected but likely and whether or not you will prepare for it.

Risk in retirement takes many forms. It is hard to pin down and define risk with confidence. Some risk can be quantified while other forms are opaque and subjective. To get a handle on what risk you should prepare for and how you should prepare for it would be to look at the various forms of risk as forms of uncertainty.

Uncertainty

The longer you live the more time you have to fill and the greater the chance of something unexpected or uncertain will happen to you. There will be stressors to your income, lifestyle and companionship. While you can't control everything, you can prepare for the likely.

Your plan gives you a sense of direction. It allows you to anticipate and react to events that affect you. It increases your control and provides you with peace of mind. It forces you to think things through so when something happens you have a sense of what to do. It helps you avoid living from crises to crises.

If you don't recognize change will happen in your life you can't plan for it. Things will happen in your life and things will happen outside your life that affects you. Your plan keeps change in perspective and provides you with options for corrective courses of action. It is like a garden. If you don't tend to it the weeds and critters take over and it becomes a mess. If you know how you want things you readily reestablish order.

Uncertainty makes planning more difficult. To simplify and make uncertainty more manageable you can separate it into three categories; predictable, risk and unpredictable.

You can view the degrees of uncertainty somewhat like weather and natural phenomena. The first degree is like the seasons, manageable. In summer you are confident it won't snow but it might rain on your parade.

The second degree is as if you live where there are tornadoes and hurricanes, there is some warning. You may or may not be directly affected, but you need to make conscious decisions each year whether or not you will prepare for them. The risk can be identified and your response readied. You may hide in the basement or batten the windows or get additional home owners' insurance.

The third degree is more like earthquakes, unpredictable. If you live in earthquake country you know one will strike. You just don't know when, where, or how severe it will be. You can choose to ignore the risk or you can set aside a few days of water and canned food and set up a telephone tree to stay in touch with your loved ones just in case.

Just because something is predictable doesn't mean it's certain. You can predict the winner of the next Super Bowl or the winner of the best actress award but you aren't always right. Predictable uncertainty takes form in your retirement plan in a number of ways. It is woven into the assumptions you make. It also shows up in events you anticipate like a child's wedding or a kitchen remodel.

One critical part of your retirement plan is to guess how much money you need to maintain your lifestyle in the years ahead. Predictable uncertainty arises when you guess wrong and you spend something different than you thought you would spend.

Predictable uncertainty is in the inflation assumptions you make. The amount of money you'll need is substantially more if you think inflation will average out to be four percent as opposed to two percent. Similarly, you'll make assumptions on how much you'll earn on your savings. If your estimate is too high you get a false sense of security while too low may overly restrict your lifestyle.

Predictably uncertainty shows up in events such as marriages, divorces, changing residences and other personal lifestyle changes. It occurs when you decide to make major expenses such as buying a new car, repairing the roof and similar large purchases.

Predictable uncertainty underlies projects you undertake. These can include things like remodeling kitchens, extensive travel, and volunteer commitments. Projects are notorious for exceeding budgets and deadlines. Events and projects shock your monthly budgets generally in one large bite in one given year.

In the first degree of uncertainty, you identify the desired or expected outcome. It usually is found in things you initiate. You tend to be a participant as opposed to a spectator in realizing its effects. Your level of control is high and the uncertain outcome is somewhat predictable in that it lies within a knowable range. Rarely will you start out to remodel your kitchen and end up with a tennis court. With enough verve, you can corral the deviations and end up with your kitchen.

The first degree of uncertainty can generally be met with detailed planning and attentive management. It has financial and social impacts that may require you to make adjustments to your plan and needs to be accounted for in the planning process.

The second degree of uncertainty tends to be random. Your control lessens and there is no clear-cut cause and effect to what you experience. This gets reflected in things like average life expectancy, chances of getting prostate cancer and whether you will get slammed by the next hurricane.

Here you enter the world of statistics and probability and think in terms of chances, likelihoods and averages. The difficulty is to determine how you, as an individual, relate to the statistic. If you can do this you can do those things that increase the chances of good things happening and decrease the chances of bad things happening.

For example, life expectancy is 79 years. What does this mean to us? It has one meaning if you are age sixty, overweight with diabetes and your parents and siblings are all dead. It has another meaning if you are 75 healthy and all of our family members lived to age 95.

The statistics reported in the media are based on the law of large numbers. They are group statistics not directly meaningful to the individual. It is like flying at forty thousand feet and seeing the Pacific Ocean as calm and appearing to be a nice day for a sail. While someone else is in a lifeboat in the same ocean dealing with twenty-foot swells and praying to all for some help. It is the same ocean at the same time.

The second degree of uncertainty acts as lord over much of your day-to-day activities. It is there in auto accidents, health diagnoses, nursing home admissions and the lottery. Your challenge is to extract meaning from the collective and apply it to you, the individual.

You can do things to change the odds like eat healthy and exercise but the desirable outcome may or may not be achieved. You keep nudging the ball towards the goal, but sometimes the goal moves. More things happen beyond your boundary of control. It's like the TV remote. It works well on your TV but no matter how hard you point it at your neighbor's TV he still watches reality shows.

The second degree of uncertainty affects how much money you need, how long you will live and whether or not you will have severe health problems. Risks that can be measured can be insured or you can choose to accept the risk yourself. There is some level of predictability through statistics that can be used to provide guidance. This risk can be managed through outside insurance or creating a rainy day fund to meet the uncertainty.

The third degree of uncertainty is the area beyond your perceived boundaries of control. This is the 'I- never- saw- that- coming' zone. This area is less about planning and more about anticipation and response. It is not random and has some cause and effect. Many of the effects are due to the interaction of people and things that create strings of unpredictability.

For example, Harry in Flint Michigan had one of those out-of-the zone experiences. Physicists studying Self Organizing Entities (SOE) observed molecules tend to gather in ways that build up an entity to a point where it collapses. The system gets overloaded and fractures in unpredictable ways.

Later studies used sand piles where the physicists dropped one grain of sand at a time onto a pile and waited for a slide or avalanche to occur. Ultimately computer models were used to see if the collapse could be predicted and if so where it would happen. The moment of collapse and the subsequent fractures are presently unpredictable.

Something like the sand pile collapse occurred in our financial system in 2008. For several years people were able to get mortgages without verifying their income and in some cases would get loans in excess of an already inflated home value. Interest rates were teasingly low so borrowers could afford the payments for a short time. Later, as interest rates rose to market rates, the borrowers could not make their payments and defaulted.

During this time, banks unloaded these toxic assets on unknowing investors duped by profit-dazed once objective rating agencies. Corrupt appraisers and mortgage brokers worked the front line. Congressional and regulatory oversight took a holiday to focus on fundraising for the upcoming elections. Grains of sand kept piling on.

The first fissure was the banks. They no longer had the capital or appetite to make loans. Ultimately, businesses convulsed and some went bankrupt. This brings us back to Harry. He worked for General Motors his entire working life. He thought the company was great and invested all of his savings in investment grade General Motor bonds. He thought he was set for life.

GM filed for bankruptcy and got a government bailout. But, for the first time in bankruptcy history, top line secured creditors were forced to the back of the bus in claiming the assets that secured their loans. Ultimately, they may get ten cents on the dollar. Harry is broke and nearly destitute. He needs to adjust his retirement plan.

The third degree of uncertainty is unpredictable. Its fractures and fissures go in all sorts of unpredictable directions. Statistical analysis does not work. It affects your retirement through your investments, your responsibilities to others and efforts in achieving your goals.

Sometimes you can only make sense of the impact of the unpredictable after the fact. It is like entering a maze. The deeper you go in the more choices you have. But at any given moment you don't know the way out or where the maze ends. If you rise above the maze you can see the routes that get you to the end.

Your current predicament may be the result of unpredictable forces. You may use reverse logic to see how you got there and find it makes sense after the fact. But at the time you made your choices you could not see the pattern that would have provided the best outcome.

Being unpredictable means something may or may not happen with the outcomes unknown at the time. This is reflected in both the effects of gradual change such as aging along with the sudden impact of something unexpected like a market collapse. You can plan for the third degree of uncertainty with an anticipation and response strategy and by hedging your outlook.

The key to thriving the three degrees of uncertainty is anticipation, preparedness and adaptability. You may think as you age you are through with adaptability but it has just changed shapes. Now, it may be more crucial than ever to be able to effectively adapt to change. Your plan needs to anticipate and react to things around you. You can do this by measuring and evaluating how things in your plan change.

Longlifers plan and manage their affairs by strictly following a specific process. By adhering to a repeatable process, they can see how things in their plan interact and can measure the affects of uncertainty in their lives. Their process provides perspective and a mechanism to adapt to these changes. They look up periodically to get a lay of the land while managing the here and now. They prepare for contingencies.

Health

Nowhere will you experience the impact of the three degrees of uncertainty than on your health. The state of your health determines how you go about your day and the activities you undertake. It affects who you hang out with and whether or not you can remain in your home. Unpleasant uncertainty in addition to altering your daily life definitely will lighten your pocketbook.

The first degree of uncertainty, predictable uncertainty, is threaded into the aging process. The body wears out over time. You will garner more aches and pains, require more doctor visits and take more prescription medications. Maintenance, both preventative and ongoing, will be required if you are to live an active life.

All of this attention requires money. Most of the expenses can be covered by your health insurance. You likely have had some form of health insurance for most of your life and going into retirement will require you maintain some level of insurance to protect your financial well being should the predictable evolve into the chronic.

The second degree of uncertainty, random uncertainty, leads you into the world of chance. Here you look at the probability of heart attacks, strokes, diabetes, cancer and other maladies. Insurance companies price their products based on those probabilities and your task is to compare your personal health status to the at-large population statistic.

Random uncertainty is where the largest health expense lay. A short stint in the hospital can readily cost into the tens of thousands of dollars. A couple of short stays or one long one can wipe out years of savings and threaten the quality of the remainder of your retired life. Insurance of some form to cover these random expenses reduces risk to your financial well being.

The third degree of uncertainty, unpredictable uncertainty, is where something may or may not happen and its impact may be minor or large. This is where something out-of-the blue imposes itself into your life.

For example, you may not think playing tennis and nursing home stays are related. What if one day you go out to play tennis and land with a thump on your right leg? You hear a pop. After an MRI you find out you tore your ACL. The surgery to repair your knee leaves you with a blood clot which finds its way to your heart.

After successful recovery from a Code Blue, you leave the ICU for a short stay in a regular hospital room before your release. The blood thinner you were given proved less than 100% effective and the clot moved through your blood stream into your head and caused a stroke. The good news is your prognosis after spending six months in a nursing home and $100,000 in uncovered expenses is hopeful and you should fully recover after nine months of physical therapy.

The best way to avoid major health expenses is to stay out of the system. You can do this by staying healthy and following the goals you set in your Personal and Others' segments of your plan. You will need to prepare for uncertainty to protect your nest egg from being ravished by the health industry.

One way to prepare is by purchasing health insurance. This appears obvious but there are a number of subtle ways the health costs can invade your nest and feast on your wealth. Nearly everyone over age 65 qualifies for Medicare the exceptions being some collective bargaining workers, some government workers and isolated pockets of people covered by other programs.

You've paid into Medicare your entire working life. So what do you get? There are four key parts to Medicare:

- Part A - (Hospital Insurance) – This helps cover inpatient hospitals, skilled nursing facilities, hospice and some home health care.
- Part B – (Medical Insurance) – This helps pay for doctors' services, outpatient care and some preventative care.
- Part C – (HMO, PPO) This includes programs run by private companies that accept Medicare payments to provide Parts A & B services.
- Part D – (Prescription Drugs) This provides coverage for prescription drug options provided by private insurance companies.

There is no monthly premium charge for Part A though you do have to pay a deductible and coinsurance amounts for hospital visits. Part B is roughly $100 a month per person and is also subject to deductibles and coinsurance. Part C generally has no premium cost unless you choose to get additional coverage. Part C tends to provide the most protection from uncovered costs but limits which doctors, hospitals and other providers you choose and can restrict services provided to you. Part D cost is roughly $40 a month and has its own set of deductibles and coinsurance.

The 2009 Trustees Report on Medicare showed the program essentially bankrupt. The 2010 report showed some improvement mostly from new Medicare taxes imposed by the 2010 health care law. Medicare's solvency has been extended to 2029 based on some overly generous assumptions in the report. One assumption is the economy will grow at 5.1% for the foreseeable future. The long-term US growth rate is roughly 3% and the report was completed in the middle of a recession.

The report also assumes doctors and hospitals would readily accept an immediate 29% cut in payments and about half the annual increase going forward. The American Medical Association responded that 20% of overall physicians and 33% of primary care doctors currently limit Medicare patients in their practice and expect to increase those limits due to the reduction in reimbursements.

The new health care law does little to control medical expenses. It essentially increases demand for services, by covering millions more people at subsidized rates, and limits supply of services by paying less than going rates. It is like squeezing a balloon. Costs may decline to the government but instead shift to patients and providers along with the potential for reduced care, longer waits and denial of coverage.

Although you have Medicare coverage, you need to be aware of the ways costs will be shifted to you as the system heads towards insolvency. The cost shift is likely to take four forms:

1. Premium increases in access of general inflation
2. Increase out-of-pocket costs
3. Reimbursement limits
4. Denial of coverage

The trustees' report stated Part B costs increased an average of 8.3% per year for the last five years. If similar increases were to hold, your monthly Part B cost would rise from $100 a month today, to over $150 a month in five years and roughly $500 a month in 20 years.

Part D drug costs have been rising at a faster 9.4% rate. This would drive the $40 a month today to over $240 a month in 20 years. Costs can't rise at such rates forever without something being done. Regardless of what gets done, the chances are you will pay more and this needs to be factored into your plan.

One health insurance study estimated the average cost for out-of-pocket expenses for retirees was $4,530 per year, per person ($377.50 per month). This included such things as vision, dental and over-the-counter drugs. It also included payments made by the retiree for health services not paid for by their insurance.

Out-of-pocket expenses in Medicare are mostly from deductibles and coinsurance. Deductibles are the amount you pay up front until you have paid some limit. Coinsurance is where the plan pays let's say 80% of the costs up to some dollar level than 100% above that dollar level. You are required to pay the 20% up to some dollar ceiling.

For example, if a hospital's bill was $3,000 you may have to pay 20% of it or $600. After you pay some maximum amount, the health plan would pick up all expenses above that level.

The risk to you is Medicare can raise the ceiling so you pay more or it can lower the amount it will pay doctor so the doctor may come to you for the difference between what Medicare pays and what the doctor or hospital wants.

What's typically done today is Medicare will say that it will only pay $1,500 of the $3,000 hospital bill. You would still pay our 20% on the lower amount for a net cost of $300 and Medicare would pay $1,200.

The hospital can shrug and accept Medicare payment as this is all it can get or it could say you are personally responsible for the difference of this $3,000 less Medicare's $1,200 and your $300 for a total additional out-of-pocket expense to you of $1,800.

This is where the hunger of the medical system quickly eats away your savings. Arbitrary caps by Medicare and a service provider who will not accept the lower rate for full payment leaving you in the lurch. You can either forego the services or pay up.

One way to deal with Medicare's cost shifting is to buy supplemental health insurance. Insurance policies that cover the gaps in Medicare coverage are known as Medigap policies. These are generally worth purchasing. The policies allow you to shift the risk of uncertain but potentially large health expenses to the insurance company for a monthly premium.

Medigap benefit plans are fixed by law. The plans are identified by letters A, B, C, D, F, G, K, L, M, and N. The gap in lettering is not a reflection of literacy but certain plans were dropped over time. Each plan has a different level of coverage. They cover different levels of deductibles, coinsurance, excess charges and such.

Although the benefits of each individual plan must be identical in coverage, the insurance company offering the plan can charge different rates. For example, Plan A with insurance company 1 and Plan A with insurance company 2 must have the same benefit levels yet each insurance company can charge different rates.

You need to decide if you want to pay a higher premium to one company over the other. Some reasons for the higher payment could be financial stability of the company, level of service or the agent is your brother-in-law. Generally, it is best to select the company offering the lowest price.

The average cost of a Medigap policy is $200 per month per person. Costs will vary geographically and by carrier. Its monthly premium is subject to annual increases and will likely mimic rising health care costs in general. Even with coverage you will still face a certain amount of out-of-pocket expenses.

Medicare, Medigap and supplemental insurance all use some for of reimbursement limits. Originally, this was to keep health providers from charging whatever they wanted. In most cases providers negotiate with insurance companies for limits on the cost of various services and limit additional costs shifted to you. But, there is an increase likelihood providers won't accept ongoing lowering of reimbursements and will seek additional payments from patients.

Denial of coverage will become a greater issue in the years ahead as the number of retirees increase. Today, coverage is denied mostly for medical necessity reasons or where there are cheaper alternatives. Some insurance companies will try to deny coverage simply because it's too expensive. Subject to the contract you have with the company you may have recourse if you are denied coverage.

The scarier trend is the shifting of denial-of-coverage to bureaucratic cost/benefit analyses. This has been popular in health policy circles as experts' at large universities and health care consulting firms view denial as a major and rational tool to reduce medical costs. Mostly, it is a form of rationing.

Imagine you are 80 years old and need hip and knee replacement surgery. The cost/benefit analysis may conclude that the costs are too high to give you a couple of years of pain free living. So to save the system, let's say $50,000, you are denied the coverage for the surgery.

This may seem cruel but imagine 80 million new retirees limping onto a bankrupt system in a country overloaded with debt and you can see the bureaucratic mindset as it tries to meet their cost cutting goals for the quarter.

Your health care costs will increase either through rising premiums, out-of-pocket costs, limit to what is covered or denial of coverage. Medigap and Medicare supplemental insurance and a rainy day fund will be necessary to maintain your quality of life and your dignity. It also helps to stay healthy and avoid the system as long as you can.

Long Term Care

Long term care, or nursing home care, is not covered by Medicare or Medigap. Those policies do cover some home health care expenses. They also cover some skilled nursing facilities' costs when the admission is related to a recent hospital stay. Nursing home care is more maintenance than prevention or repair and thus is not covered by health insurance.

You should be convinced you need health insurance. As you age there is a high probability you will need health care and a high probability that it will cost a lot. But, do you need Long Term Care (LTC) insurance?

LTC risk behaves differently than health risk. LTC, although it doesn't have a theoretical limit, it does have a practical limit. Rarely will you stay more than two or three years. This serves as a practical cap on what you might have to pay should you not have LTC insurance.

Most nursing home stays are for less than 90 days and few last longer than two years. If you were to stay in a nursing home for the full two years you could pay a total of $200,000. This may be out of reach for some people, for others it could cause severe hardship. Still others may easily pay this amount from their savings.

Costs of LTC tend to be smaller than health costs and tend to be spread over time. If you went into a nursing home you most likely would pay, depending where you live, between $2,000 and $9,000 a month.

Paying monthly gives you a chance to redirect your current income or sell some assets in a rational manner. It does not cause an immediate financial catastrophe.

In contrast, even a short hospital stay with minor surgery could easily exceed what you would pay in total for nursing home care. The hospital bill needs to be paid immediately while the nursing home can be paid over time. An uninsured hospital stay could wipe you out financially while an uninsured nursing home stay gives you time to come up with payment options.

The purchase of LTC insurance is perplexing. New retirees entering the new retirement have a choice of using a chunk to their monthly budget today and maybe never need care or take a hit to their savings tomorrow should they need care and lack coverage.

The contracts are complex, confusing and costly. To add to the difficulty in making a decision you need to balance the emotional value, your feeling of security in being covered, with the rational value of the insurance premium.

Philosophers, at least since Plato, debated the dominance of the rational mind versus the emotional mind. The argument continues to this day. Recently, scientific studies have been able to identify and measure activity in the parts of the brain associated with the rational and emotional components.

Their studies concluded that neither side is preferable in all decision-making activities. The rational side is better in some types of decision making and the emotional side in others.

When decisions affect you personally, as opposed to something in the external environment, you need to access both the rational and the emotional parts of your brain. This becomes evident when you attempt to make a variety of retirement decisions.

Long term care insurance qualifies as the poster child for this dual decision-making approach. If your decisions tend towards the emotional/intuitive than you feel the fear of staying in a nursing home, the loss of independence and the lack of dignity strongly and would tend to overpay for insurance.

If you are a rational/calculating person you may discount your feelings about staying in a nursing home and bluster about finishing your life in your home. You think the likelihood of entering a nursing home is smaller than it truly is and consequently not worth making premium payments today. You would tend to self or under-insure. How should you go about making a decision?

First, look to the likelihood of needing the insurance then determine what it will likely cost. Then you can use your internal calculus, your emotional decision maker, to see if it is worth it. Though the cost may be the same for two individuals, the emotional calculation may be different where one person sees it as a deal and the other as too costly. Both are right. But, first determine the true economic cost.

The California Department of Health Services reports there is a 40% chance of spending some time in a nursing home. 90% of stays are for one year or less. You should consider these statistics when you contemplate the purchase of policies with coverage lasting multiple years or lifetime.

The report further states that 64% of the stays in a nursing home are for less than 2 months. These stays tend to be the result of suffering an event that initially lands you in the hospital but you end up in a treatment zone where you are not sick enough to stay in the hospital and are too sick to go home. This is one of the areas not covered by Medicare or Medigap insurance.

The average cost for stay in a nursing home nationwide is $50,000 per year. But, in major cities the cost is more than double. New York City the cost is $140,708, San Francisco $97,820 and the ten biggest cities in the country are all over $80,000. These costs tend to increase faster than inflation. But, to get decent care from qualified people, in a major urban area $100,000 is a good starting point for what you can expect to pay.

In statistics there is a concept of expected value. Expected value is what something is expected to cost or pay out multiplied by the probability of it happening. To apply this to nursing homes costs you would multiply the chance of going into the nursing home times its costs.

To get a sense of the dollar risk you take the 40% chance of going to a nursing home times the average $100,000 cost to get coverage from day one. You would be willing to pay a total of $40,000 in premiums (100,000*.4). This number serves as a reference point for the most you would be willing to pay.

In a typical LTC policy a 40 year-old paying annual premiums and begins using the insurance at age 80 will pay about $22,000 over the forty year period, a fifty year old will pay $29,320 and a sixty year old will pay $50,000 in premiums prior to using the insurance at age 80. To get a value the total premiums paid should be less than the expected cost.

Another way to look at this is to assume you will enter a nursing home at age 80. This is when most stays begin. Therefore, if you are 60 today you would be willing to pay up to $2,000 per year for 20 years to get coverage ($2,000 times 20 equals $40,000). You then can make an internal judgment and balance a $2,000 a year payment with the emotional value you attach to offloading nursing home cost risk.

Even if the policy is cost effective, it still may not make sense for a number of people to buy it. You also need to look at the impact of the premium and uninsured nursing home costs on your income and your savings.

If you are wealthy you may be able to afford to pay the $100,000 without affecting your lifestyle, then it may be best to self insure. Especially, since 64% of stays are for less than two month the likelihood is you would not incur the full $100,000. But, if the emotional side of you prefers to eliminate this risk than purchasing a cost-effective policy may be worth it to you.

At the opposite end of the wealth scale, if the premium payments would impoverish you, you should consider not purchasing LTC and opt for Medicaid or State sponsored coverage. Selecting government support limits your choices of where you get coverage and most likely the care would not be as good as at the facilities that charge more. But, you will not feel the financial drain today for something that may not happen tomorrow.

This leaves the middle class as the most likely to consider LTC. If your wealth is under $1 million the impact of an extended stay in a nursing home could quickly deplete your resources. Imagine coughing up an extra $5,000 -$8,000 a month for a number of months.

Not only will you have the additional expense, but you also lose income off the money you pay for the services. To make matters worse, you may have to take taxable income to pay for these expenses if you draw the funds from your IRA or by taking capital gains.

You need to look at the premium cost and the likely impact on your savings before making a decision. If your health and durability are questionable the chances of needing care will be greater than average than the coverage may be a deal.

If you are healthy and not inclined to purchase insurance at any cost, you still should make a conscious note of the impact on your savings should you need care and lack coverage. You can set up a rainy-day portion of your savings for this degree of uncertainty in your overall plan.

LTC cost like most other health care costs, are increasing faster than inflation. These costs could easily triple in the 20-30 years we will spend in retirement. If you postpone the purchase, there is the possibility you may get sick and no longer qualify for the coverage.

The decision to buy LTC is both emotional and financial and you each need to find your own balance of whether you want to shift the risk to an insurance company or self insure.

Throughout your retirement, you will face different forms of risk and uncertainty. Your ability to manage this uncertainty depends on your being aware of it. The POISE process allows you to review your position in a structured fashion. This helps you to intelligently assess and respond to new levels of uncertainty.

Chapter 12

LEGACY

In the consolidation and contemplation stages of retirement, the notion of how your life will be viewed by others strengthens. Each of us seems to have an inner drive to live a life of meaning. There is a sense of importance to leave something behind.

The measure of our lives in many ways is calculated on how we have helped others. Your drive may be toward family, or it may be toward the community at large. It may be a combination. This measure becomes your legacy.

Your legacy consists of your life actions and of how you ultimately dispose of your worldly possessions. In the early stages of retirement, you will get a sense of the level of your financial security. You will also be able to set the foundation for your legacy through your Personal and Other goals.

While you set the tone and direction of your retirement, there are some final tasks all responsible people need to complete; nothing seems to be truly finished until all the paperwork has been done.

You need to give instructions for your personal care should you become incapacitated. You need to let others know how you wish to dispose of your personal belongings and your wealth. Although much of this is unpleasant to think about, it becomes the final working task of your overall retirement plan.

If you do nothing, either by choice or procrastination, you leave all decisions to the laws of the state where you reside. The way the state will take care of you should you become incapacitated may differ wildly from your own wishes. Similarly, how your possessions get distributed will not likely match the way you would like to see them distributed.

For example, in most states, if you are married and die without a will or a trust, your assets are split among your spouse and children. Everything of your does not automatically go to your spouse, only those things where you share title. In some cases, your wealth can be distributed beyond your immediate family to siblings, cousins and so on.

Doing nothing leaves a mess behind for others to clean up. It opens your affairs to fights among your heirs and relatives while the attorneys, accountants, and administrators feast on your estate.

Doing something brings you into the world of estate planning. Estate planning is the paperwork you need to have in place to protect yourself and your property while you are alive and to ensure your instructions for distributing your property are followed.

ESTATE PLANNING

Phase I: Personal Care

In the first phase, you protect yourself and your savings in the case of disability and incapacitation through durable powers-of-attorney. These are documents where you designate who you will give signing power to handle your affairs should you become incapacitated.

In most states, your spouse does not have automatic authority to buy, sell, or distribute your property without your consent. You would have to create a power-of-attorney to give this authority to your spouse or some other loved one to act on your behalf.

The powers you give can be limited in duration and to property, or they can be broad and unlimited to cover cases of mental incapacity. Obviously, whoever you name you need to trust as they have complete access to your savings.

You might want one of your children to handle your financial affairs at some later age when bill paying, taxes and general money management gets to be too much of a burden.

If a disability is sudden and extreme, the durable power-of-attorney can prevent delays in you getting the necessary attention you need as providers of care worry about their liability and what services they can legally provide.

The person with this authority acts on your behalf. Financial resources and legal decisions can be made on your behalf quickly and cost-effectively. If you recover and are competent enough to resume the management of your affairs, the power-of-attorney gets suspended and you are back in action.

Another critical document is a durable power-of-attorney for health care. This is also known in some states as a living will. This document tells the medical community that you do not want end-of-life heroics. If you end up in a coma or near death, this document gives your permission to them to stop treatment.

If you do not want end-of-life support, a copy of this document should be held by your personal physician and in your records at the hospital where you are most likely would be treated.

These documents tend to have expiration dates. They are usually good for two years. If you choose to have one of these documents, make it part of your annual planning review to make sure it is up to date.

Both the standard durable power-of-attorney and the living will documents are available for free on the Internet. They are basically fill-in-the-blank forms but may require you to have your signature witnessed or notarized. If you have doubts or complex affairs, then you should consult with an attorney.

If you are married or have a life partner, some additional planning may be required to take care of the spouse. If you are the one generating the most income from Social Security, pensions and annuities and your survivor is dependent on these funds, then you need to take your distributions jointly.

You start out with a lower monthly benefit, but the benefit continues to pay over both of your lives. Your spouse would still get income should you die first. Another alternative is the use of life insurance where your spouse gets the death proceeds to supplement their income.

Most families delegate tasks. If financial management is one of those tasks delegated to one spouse, the other spouse needs to prepare for doing this work alone. If you are the one responsible for the financial management of your household, you need to consider how your spouse would manage these affairs without you.

You can teach your spouse or you could bring in an outside financial advisor while you both are alive. This gives you the opportunity to build trust with the advisor and have that person understand you family needs. The surviving spouse has time to build a comfort level in the financial management of your household.

Your spouse should also have a basic understanding of the financial management process. Knowing how things are supposed to work helps with catching things out-of-the-ordinary. The POISE process provides the checks and balances to make it difficult for your surviving spouse to be exploited.

Phase II: Property

If you do not have instructions in place, no one knows where you want your stuff to go. They will not know how to distribute your personal belongs or your savings. The easiest way to make your intentions known is to create a basic will.

This can simply be a handwritten and witnessed set of instructions. Or it can be an elaborate document, listing how everything you own will be distributed along with any conditions you might want to apply.

If you are reluctant to see a lawyer, standard, simple will forms are also available on the Internet for free. More sophisticated versions of will are available for a cost at many legal websites.

If you have complex assets like a closely held business, investment real estate or corporations and such, these forms generally will not suffice. Nor will they if you have complex family matters.

If you have minor age, irresponsible, or disable children, you need a more sophisticated will. If you think your heirs will have disagreements and potentially fight over the estate, then you need a more sophisticated will. You will need to consult with a lawyer to get one properly drafted.

In your will, you will need to name an executor or administrator of your estate. This person would oversee all the things necessary to close out your affairs. Wills are required to be presented in probate court to make the final distributions. Your executor will need to hire an attorney to complete the probate process.

Wills are usually not that expensive to set up. But settling your estate will require lawyer and court costs. The records from probate are considered public records. This gives curious people access to all your previously private information.

The process in most states lasts six months from the date the will is filed with the probate court not from the date of death. It may take some time for your grieving heirs to get your affairs organized, hire an attorney, and begin the process.

In many cases, heirs may not have access to their inheritance for a year or more. Some large estates can be held in administrative limbo for five, ten years, or more. Meanwhile, legal, accounting, and administration fees mount up.

To avoid the costs and delays of probate, many people create revocable living trusts. These usually supplement simple wills. The will becomes the document to pass on your intentions and your personal property like jewelry, mementos, and such. It would also include a provision to pour-over assets you did not get to put into your living trust for distribution purposes.

The revocable living trust manages the distribution of your savings and wealth. Assets can begin to be distributed immediately. Since the trusts are revocable, you can change them during your life since you are the initial trustee. If things change in your life, you can still make any changes you like.

Living trusts are a bit more complicated and more expensive to set up. You would name a successor trustee – in most cases, one of your children - to manage the distribution of your estate. You would need to change title on your assets from how they are now held to the name of your living trust.

One of the biggest mistakes many people make is they create a living trust but do not change the title on their properties and accounts to the name of the trust. This defeats the purpose of the trust.

Your living trust can serve as an overarching trust for many sub-trusts serving specialized purposes. Currently, each person is entitled to an estate tax credit that allows a certain value of property to pass to your heirs free of estate tax.

If you are married, you need to create a specific provision to retain your credit. If you pass your entire portion of your estate to your spouse without using this special provision, then you lose your credit. Your spouse has only one credit left to shelter the estate from estate taxes.

The estate tax laws seem to change with each new presidential administration. The estate tax credit tends to range from $5 -$10 million per person. Which means you would only pay estate taxes on amounts greater than the credit. The estate tax rate also varies and generally is between 45 -55 percent.

Considering the financial condition of the country, there is great uncertainty as to what the future credit will be. It is likely that sometime during your retirement, you will need to consider additional planning to minimize the effect of the tax on your estate.

Other sub-trusts under your living trust umbrella could be set up to hold money for minor children. Children under age eighteen cannot own property. This means that if you want to be certain your gifts to your children or grandchildren are restricted solely for their use, you would need to convert these gifts into a trust for them.

Sub-trusts can also be used for adult children to protect them from themselves. Some may not be mature or savvy enough to manage their financial affairs when sums get large. Some may see this largesse as a windfall and spend it in a wanton fashion. The surprise comes in how quickly this gift disappears.

Passing very large amounts of money to the next generation can hinder their motivation. Having their physical needs met, they wander aimlessly through life. Many heirs of large estates have a higher likelihood of drug addiction, alcoholism, and divorce.

One of your final parental duties is to thoroughly think through how each of your children would handle their portion of your estate. If the sum is large, at least in the mind of your children, you can spread the distributions over time. They could get some immediately, some at age 40, and the balance at age 45 or some later age.

Some set their distribution of their estate to provide their children with money at retirement age. This ensures the kids continue to work productively have a fail-safe should things go awry.

Another common sub-trust is a special-needs trust for disabled children. This trust holds wealth for the child's benefit but preserves the child's access to government benefits. The funds could be used to provide a better level of housing, personal care, and other quality-of-life benefits.

Living trusts are quite flexible and can be tailored to meet a variety of needs you may have in the distribution of your estate. You can design it to support your legacy or use it to efficiently administer the distribution of your wealth.

Not everything you own may be titled in your trust. Some holdings like IRAs, 401(k)s, and similar pension holdings come under different property laws and cannot be owned by personal trusts.

These assets get distributed through your beneficiary designations. Life insurance and annuities are also distributed by beneficiary designation. However, you can make your trust the beneficiary if certain rules are followed.

Beneficiary distributions avoid probate. But problems can arise if your trust is not the beneficiary. The beneficiary gets the money separate from your trust instructions. Your beneficiary designations need to be coordinated with your trust distributions to ensure each of your heirs gets what you want them to get.

If you do not coordinate them, one problem could be that one child gets the assets through a beneficiary designation and the other the costs of closing your estate through the trust. This could lead to unequal or unintended consequences, leaving the children to fight it out. In some cases, people do not update their beneficiaries, leaving an old designation on the books.

The surviving spouse could get quite a surprise, finding out that certain IRA assets are going to the ex-spouse or some other beneficiary, bypassing the surviving spouse completely. The review of your beneficiary designations needs to be part of your retirement review process.

There may be restrictions on some property you own, and it may not be transferable to your living trust. This could include closely held business interests, certain real estate, and other business-type holdings like partnerships, joint tenancy, patents and royalties.

This restricted property gets distributed according to agreements particular to those arrangements. In most cases, the ultimate value of your holdings can get passed to your trust for distribution. If not, then you need to coordinate these distributions with your other distributions.

Your basic estate plan should consist of the following:

- Pour-over will
- Power of attorney
- Living will or health directive
- Revocable living trust (for most people/otherwise a standard will)

To get these documents properly prepared, you need to list your assets and note how they are currently titled. You need to verify your beneficiary designations to make sure they are up to date. Finally, you need to coordinate distributions to your heirs from your different holdings.

If your wealth gets to the level where it could be subject to estate taxes, additional planning may be required. If this is your case, you would need to seek professional guidance as this gets complicated quickly.

Generally, you would plan to get growth out of your estate and get the value of the remaining estate reduced for estate tax purposes. Family limited partnerships, family limited liability corporations, offshore trusts, and other legal entities help shift value around but let you retain a distant level of control. The money you decide to leave to charity is out of your estate for tax purposes.

Philanthropy and various forms of charitable giving are not only for the very wealthy. Although there are financial incentives to give some of your estate away, many people feel a need to make gifts to charity for purely philanthropic reasons. There are intelligent ways to do this.

Charitable Giving

As a species, we have an innate need to help and give to our tribe, our family. It is programmed into our DNA and is a means for survival. We feel good when we see our child smile upon receiving a sought-after holiday gift.

Our heart warms when someone we have helped displays sincere gratitude. Our brains' feel-good natural chemicals wash through us to reinforce this behavior. It just seems to be the right thing to do.

We share the things of sustenance and sacrifice a modicum of immediate gratification to share with those we love. When we move beyond our tribe and family and share and give to others, we discover philanthropy. An examined life requires some form of charity, some way of helping others.

Scientific studies show that we are in tune to those around us. When someone is fearful, we feel more attentive, and out fight-or-flight response gets activated. When someone is happy, we wish to get closer to them and share in the happiness. When someone is suffering, we feel empathy. Our first impulse is to help, but sometimes this impulse is overturned by our rational mind and we withhold assistance.

Intelligent charitable giving is the balance of the emotional impulse to do what is right and the rational calculation to do the right thing. You have time, knowledge, and money to share with others to build a better community.

The giving of your time and knowledge are quite straightforward. You can volunteer with countless nonprofits to provide assistance through an existing structured organization. You can identify unmet community needs and organize people and resources to help those needs.

Another form of charitable giving is to give money. This can be as simple as writing a check or handing a few dollars to a worthy cause. Once you start to look at giving larger sums of money, you need to understand the financial impact on your personal affairs. You need to look at income and estate tax considerations and how the gift will impact your future needs.

To make intelligent gifts, you separate giving into three components: current giving, testamentary giving, and planned giving. Each meets a different aspect of your emotional need to give and your rational need to give intelligently.

Current giving generally includes cash or checks but can also include property. You give without expecting anything in return other than potential recognition and a tax deduction.

Obviously, once you have made this gift, you no longer have the proceeds available for your personal uses. Subsequently, these gifts tend to be smaller in nature as what is given is what you can afford.

Cash is the most financially expensive form of gifting. In order for you to get cash to give, you must pay income taxes on some larger amount first. The cash may come from receiving a paycheck, dividends, interest, or other forms of taxable income.

You can also give property. Generally, it is more effective financially to give appreciated property such as stocks. You can give real property such as real estate, art, and business interests subject to certain conditions.

If you give appreciated property, the charity can sell the property and get the proceeds without paying taxes. In most cases, you get to avoid the capital gains tax on the appreciation and get an income tax deduction.

Testamentary Giving

This type of gift comes from your will or trust and is given to charity upon your death. You can make larger gifts as you no longer need the money. You can give all sorts of money and property subject to the charity being willing to accept it. The trade-off comes from what you leave your heirs and what you give to charity.

There is less donor recognition from testamentary gifts. You can tell a charity you will make a gift, but they know you can always change your mind. The act of providing for charity in your will gives you a sense of doing something of value, and you can direct the money to causes dear to you. It highlights and underscores the final part of your overall legacy.

Planned Giving

This tends to be the most complex form of giving. It is a hybrid, bridging current and testamentary giving. It allows you to make a large gift today where you indirectly control the gift while you are alive, with the promise that it will go to charity after your death.

In many cases, you are able to get current income and estate tax deductions today. With certain types of planned gifts, you can also get income for life.

Planned gifts allow you to make much larger gifts as you hedge the potential that you may need the benefits from this wealth during the remainder of your life. There are many forms of planned giving, but the four most popular are the following:

- *Charitable Remainder Trust.* These trusts are generally set up for life. You contribute appreciated property to the trust, and the trust sells the property and is exempt from capital gains taxes. You have control over the proceeds and are given a specified income for life. You get a partial income tax deduction and an estate tax deduction. Upon death, whatever remains in the trust goes to the charity of your choice.
- *Charitable Gift Annuities.* Gift annuities are contracts directly entered into with a qualified charity. You contribute cash or appreciated property in exchange for lifetime income. You get a partial income tax deduction, deferral of capital gains taxes and an estate tax deduction. However, you do not get to control the investments.
- *Private Foundation.* Money or property is set aside in a legal structure to benefit society. When you establish a foundation,

you are considered a custodian of public wealth and are subject to a variety of rules and regulations. You get a current income tax deduction, avoid capital gains taxes on contributed property and get an estate tax deduction. You have control over the wealth and can direct it however you see fit as long as you follow the rules. You must give away at least 5 percent a year. If the foundation earns more on its investments, the foundation can go on indefinitely. Foundations can be complex and costly to run but offer you control and a certain status in society.

- *Donor Advised Funds.* Existing charities formed under specific tax rules can accept donations and set them aside for you to make future gifts. In some cases, you can advise on how the proceeds are invested. You get the income tax deduction today but can postpone the ultimate distribution of the gift to some future time. You can avoid capital gain taxes on contributed property and get an estate tax deduction. The gift fund mimics aspects of a private foundation without the legal restrictions and high set up and operating costs but offers you less control.

Taxes being taxes, the use of deductions comes with restrictions and complexities. It is not a simple matter to give wealth away and take a tax deduction for it. Larger gifts require planning for the financial impact to your life, along with ensuring that you follow the rules to get the tax benefits.

You can make larger gifts than you thought possible by exploring the creative ways to give. You can tap your need for philanthropy, enhance your legacy, and maybe make society just a bit better.

Your legacy will be determined by your actions and interactions with your family and community at large. You have time, money, and intent at your disposal to paint a picture of how your life will be remembered.

Chapter 13

SUSTAINABILITY

The government, business and overall economy will shift cost, risk and uncertainty to you throughout your retirement. The old, predictable, stable system of generations past will crumble and erode as the new hoard-of-retirees pounce on it. The new system has yet to be defined. Somehow, you will need to manager your way through the gap.

Clouds, thunder and lightening appear on the horizon. The atmospherics of fiscal irresponsibility, global economic competition and political gridlock power the storm. The time where borrowing money was easier than cutting spending or raising taxes has ended. Tough decisions will need to be made if we are to avert economic collapse.

The U.S. is over 100 percent of its annual income and growing rapidly. The growth rate of new debt exceeds the growth in the economy. This is like you earning $100,000 per year and having $110,000 in credit card debt. If you follow the government's lead, you would continually overspend your income. How long do you think this could last?

The artificially low Federal Reserve interest rate since 2008 make carrying this debt doable for the government for a short period of time. One study shows if interest rates reset to their normal long-term rate, simply paying the interest on the debt would consume over forty percent of the annual budget.

Going forward, you would have to count on someone to continuously be willing to loan you more money. At some point, you must reach a limit.

The U.S. government seems to be close to its limit of reckless spending and tax policies. The AAA rating of the government has been brought into question by S&P and Moody's rating services. A Chinese rating service has already cut its rating on U.S. debt.

Once the Federal Reserve stops printing money, the government will have to go to the global markets to find money to fund its debt. The current deficit is over $1.5 trillion per year. The government projects this deficit for as long as the eye can see. Additionally, new debt will need to be issued to cover maturing debt.

Nearly every government entity is running deficits or piling on debt. State and local governments and non-government organizations like Fannie Mae and the Pension Benefit Guaranty Corporation are financially troubled.

Pensions and retiree medical care are severely under-funded. All of these ongoing deficits will need financing along with Social Security and Medicare as new retirees stake their claim.

The Chinese have announced that they are at their limit of $1.2 trillion of U.S. Treasury debt and plan to systematically lower this. They and other countries are conducting more US-dollar trade in other currencies. The rest of the world is becoming more reluctant to hold US dollars as their reserve currency as the dollar loses value.

Europe has a massive debt problem. Greece and other countries neared default and needed bailout financing. China itself is has debt nearly three times its annual income. Japan over two times its annual income.

Large US-based mutual funds have publicly stated their lack of interest in buying more U.S. debt at these low rates. If other potential lenders feel the same way, it may not be long before we see interest rates rise, and rise swiftly.

The United States faces health care, retiree and interest costs rising faster than the growth of the economy. Its ability to continue to borrow its way out of fiscal mismanagement is checked by those unwilling to lend it more money. It is unsustainable.

It is also unavoidable that there won't be some cuts in benefits and some tax increases. The United States can increase taxes on the wealthy to 100 percent, and the amount collected would be less than the annual budget deficit.

It could confiscate all of their wealth, and it would barely cover two years of deficit. If taxes are to be increased to solve this problem, the increase would have to go deep into the middle class.

Budget battles are just beginning. The real pressure will come during the storm as four million new retirees leave the workforce each year and claim their Medicare and Social Security.

While all of this is alarming, it is still manageable. Our political process needs adult supervision. It needs the steady hand of even-tempered grown-ups. However, they seem to be in short supply.

You will need to be alert to change. Your bailout is not coming. You may be able to get what is promised you but you certainly will not get any more.

You will be more dependent on your savings. Yet the financial markets will get riskier as the United States itself becomes riskier. The new financial regulations have not gone far enough to prevent the next set of too-big-to-fail bank bailouts, adding more risk to your investment portfolio.

In this dynamic swirling environment, you will need to actively manage your retirement to stay afloat. To do this you need a systematic process to ensure its sustainability. The POISE process helps you make adjustments over the stages of retirement.

Drawdown Ratio

If your drawdown ratio is uncomfortably high, there are still some things you can do. These things center about lowering your expenses and increasing your income. You still have some options to consider:
- Move to a low-cost, low-tax state
- Move to a smaller house

- Move abroad
- Reduce lifestyle cost
- Consider a reverse mortgage
- Work longer

The first three options require you to move. This in itself may not be viable. Although if you are in a high-tax state, a move to a state without income taxes and with low property taxes could save you 5-10 percent a year in lower costs. The savings could be the difference you need to continue your desired lifestyle.

If you move to a smaller house, you may or may not stay in your current area. The move should lower your monthly costs and could free up equity in your house. The additional cash could be invested to provide additional income. A smaller house, condo, or retirement living facility frees you from a variety of work and maintenance a larger house requires.

If you are adventurous, you could move to a low-cost country. There are many expatriate communities scattered throughout the world. These communities provide a level of support to make the transition easier. Depending on the country, you could lower your monthly costs by 15-30 percent.

Southern Europe and the Caribbean could offer a lower-cost retirement, but it would be more expensive than those other countries. Yet they offer a sense of familiarity.

Before moving to another country, you should plan an extended visit to see if it works for you. Staying for several months lets you get into the rhythm of the country. The blinders of happy vacation thoughts get replaced by the day-to-day lifestyle. If you cannot make it a few months, you certainly will regret moving there.

You need to check on banking and tax policies. Some countries impose a tax on all deposits including your Social Security check. There will also be currency exchange fees to convert your dollars to the local currency.

Other countries, more friendly to expatriates, have no income or capital gains taxes. There may be restrictions on how you can own property and you should search for honest legal representation.

You most likely will need to buy some sort of supplemental health insurance. Generally, Medicare does not cover health costs in another country. You need to consider still keeping Medicare if you come back to the U.S. for treatment. Most U.S. private policies have restrictions on foreign care and limit coverage to emergencies.

There may still be some cost cutting you can do. You might want to get rid of a car or two as you will likely be driving less. Shop your home and auto insurance annually. Scrutinize all investment fees and charges. You may qualify for a variety of assistance available to low-income seniors for energy, utility, food and other related costs.

Your expense and activity plan, along with the CPR approach to expense management, should help guide you to a lower-cost retirement.

Reverse mortgages could work for certain people over age 62. These are usually a last-resort option to get additional cash. Essentially, you sign over your home to a bank in return for a lump sum of cash or a line-of-credit based on the equity in your house. You would then use this money to supplement your other income.

The bank lays claim to your equity as you consume the money you have been loaned. You don't have to pay the bank back until you sell your house. You still get to live in the house as long as you like.

There are limits and a lot of rules you need to follow to make sure you remain qualified. You still need to pay property taxes, insurance and maintenance. Generally, the up-front costs are high, eating away at your equity. There are restrictions on how you can transfer the remaining value, if any, of the property at death.

If you are nearing retirement and your drawdown ratio is high, you need to consider staying on the job. There are a number of advantages for each additional year you work. You keep your employee benefits. Your salary can pay your expenses, and consequently, you don't need to draw down your savings. Your savings have an additional year to grow.

You can add money to your savings or pay down debt for another year. Each year you work is one less year your money needs to last. As you get older, you can tolerate a higher drawdown ration. This all comes with the cost of you giving up a year of leisure and taking on the burden of work for another year.

If your current job is unbearable, you can consider doing some type of work you would enjoy even if it is for less money. The additional work and money can help you transition to a more stable retirement. You might see if your current employer has flexibility in the number of hours you work. You might be able to shift to flextime or part-time.

Embrace Retirement

If your numbers and timing align, retirement can be the best phase of your life. Work pressures dissipate. You no longer feel the push to further your career. Your children should be independent. You now have time to do all the things you have been putting off. There are a number of things you can do:

- Downshift work
- Start a business
- Volunteer
- Stay stimulated

It is hard to go from working fifty hours a week and getting a lot of attention to sitting around the house. Some of you may be ready for the downtime, others need time to adjust. You may need to stay engaged but just not so tightly.

It may be time to shift to a lower gear. This could be viewed as 'cool-down' time similar to the slower pace runners use after a long run. Having something to do eases the pressure of having nothing to do; at least until you are ready.

Many new retirees look to a second career. This work, in most cases, pays less but is enjoyed more. A number of universities now offer educational courses structured around second careers. You may have been a high-level manager but now would like to teach pre-school. Or maybe you want to develop your culinary skills. You might want to sell real estate or help other retirees with the complications of moving abroad.

Some universities offer experienced leaders the course structure to pursue advanced leadership studies. These are intensive programs allowing the students to continue their service at a high level. You would be able to instill community and public-sector organizations with new ideas and talent. The pay would be less but the level of engagement would be at the highest levels of these organizations.

You can start a new business. Your might have leadership and management skill that small start-up companies may need on a consulting basis. If you have health, accounting, computer skills or similar talents you can join temporary help agencies and work when you feel like it. Or maybe you have a great idea for a new product the market is just dying to buy.

There is always a need for volunteers at non-profit organizations. You can bring in a high level of skills and help an organization with marketing, finance or computerizing their systems. You may be able to get involved in designing and expanding services to the needy or elderly. You still have time to do something of significance and have a positive impact on your community.

It's important to stay physically, mentally and socially active. If you live out in the suburbs, retirement may seem constricting as there may be few people around to socialize with and to do anything requires a drive. You might be tired of inner city living with the high cost and crime.

Many new retirees look to different types of retirement living communities. They don't want to be labeled as living in a retirement home as that is for old people. There are a number of new living arrangements that could keep you stimulated and active.

Affinity communities allow retirees to live in groups centered about a key interest. The communities cover all sorts of interests. There are communities that are college centered where the retirees can attend local college classes and keep intellectual discussions going with other residents.

There are RV groups and Tai Chi groups. Some center about ethnic similarities others around sexual orientation. You can join golf or artist communities. America has groups for nearly everything imaginable. These groups allow you to pursue an interest and share it with others who are equally interested.

Certain areas are becoming 'naturally occurring retirement regions' (NORC)s. The NORC model offers umbrella services for retirees living in a specific region. The services reinforce community to ensure retirees don't become isolated. They help with health issues, provide social gatherings and cultural enrichment activities.

You can redefine retirement. You can choose where to live and who to hang out with. You can stay engaged in work activities or just pursue your leisure interests. The time is open and the opportunities near unlimited.

The world is open for exploration. Sitting around doing nothing is a choice. It's time to redefine or refine your retirement lifestyle. You can create your ideal Longlifer. The new retirement becomes the 'renewment'.

You can use the POISE process to reassure yourself that you are personally, socially, and financially on track. It's a matter of periodic planning, projecting, and evaluating your way through the storm.

You now have a basic set of tools and a strategy of how to navigate the retirement storm. With a little time and effort, you can free yourself from worry and get on with enjoying the next phase of your life.